DEBUNK IT!

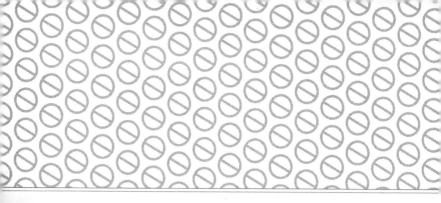

DE

HOW TO ST

JOHN GRANT

BUNK IT!

AY SANE IN A WORLD OF MISINFORMATION

ZEST BOOKS
San Francisco

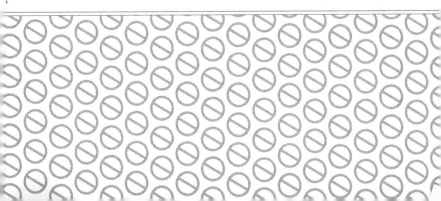

DEDICATION

This is for all the world's Franklins, but in particular it's for Tom Crowther: the best kid in the world . . . at least since his mom grew up.

Connect with Zest!

- zestbooks.net/blog
- zestbooks.net/contests
- twitter.com/zestbooks
- facebook.com/BooksWithATwist

35 Stillman Street, Suite 121, San Francisco, CA 94107 / www.zestbooks.net

Manufactured in the U.S.A.
DOC 10 9 8 7 6 5 4 3 2 1
4500513963

CONTENTS

INTRODUCTION

Let me tell you a story . . .

For good or ill, I've written a number of books about how people misunderstand science, graft their own loopy ideas onto it, or try to distort it so they can pretend it says one thing when it's really saying something else. Because of these books, I get invited from time to time to speak at libraries and schools, rationalist societies, book clubs, science fiction conventions—you name it. What usually happens is that, first, I give my carefully prepared spiel, and then the *interesting* part of the event starts, which is the question-and-answer session.

At one of these events—in which I had explained how some people were trying to use the pretense of academic freedom to get Creationism taught in school science classes—a young man named Franklin, aged maybe fourteen or fifteen, said, "What we kids need is a sort of guide to bullshit." All too often, he went on, young people are in a situation where some adults are telling them one thing is true while others are telling them quite the opposite. If they go online to try to find out the truth, it often gets even worse. "It'd be cool if there was a book not just poking holes in some of the anti-science crap people try to get us to believe, but also telling us how to tell the bullshit from the good stuff."

There were quite a few things for me to learn from his few short sentences, the most important of which was that the world could do with a whole lot more Franklins—whether in Congress, in the media, teaching, or even (and this struck a bit close to home) writing books. It's not young people who spread stupid ideas about science, after all, but older ones. And, as he'd told me, it can be hard for younger people to sort out the reality from the trash, the genuine information from the stuff that people are just making up because it suits their political beliefs, or because it's more comforting to believe a lie than face an unpalatable truth, or simply because sometimes dealing with problems requires getting up off the couch and *doing* something, so it's easier to pretend those problems don't exist.

I wanted to catch up with Franklin afterward to ask him if I could steal his idea, but by the time I was able to start looking for him he'd gone. So, wherever you are, Franklin, this book is for you—along with my heartiest thanks.

$$\oslash$$

Now, here's a question for you: How do you know the above story isn't bullshit?

How do you know I didn't just invent it? I've written lots of fantasy stories, after all. How can you tell this isn't just another one?

Well, some parts of the story are easy enough to check. You can find out through Wikipedia or Goodsearch or the online *Encyclopedia of Science Fiction* that I do indeed write those science books. It might take a little longer, but you should be able to find evidence that I've given talks on subjects like science denial to various groups. But, unless you happened to have been there that night, you're never going to know for sure if Franklin said those things or even if there *was* a Franklin. Maybe it was some other guy who made those remarks, or maybe I've pieced them together from what a lot of different people have said to me during question-and-answer sessions, or just in general conversation. Who knows?

And I'm not about to tell you, because it doesn't matter. What's important is the fact that this tale—whether true or false—is basically indistinguishable from the many tricks dishonest people use when they realize they can't produce evidence or a rational argument in defense of their position. The trick is misdirection. Although it's obviously of vital significance to Franklin and his parents whether or not he exists, it doesn't make much difference *here*. Ignoring the minor, inconsequential facts and concentrating instead on the actual *substance* of what someone's telling you is an easy tool you can use to defend yourself against bullshit. If that main point checks out, or at least if enough of it does, then maybe, just *maybe*, they're telling you the truth—or at least the truth as they know it. And that's a start.

🚫

Here's an old saying: The trouble with having an open mind is that people come along and put things in it. It's like when someone puts a Dumpster at the side of the road because they're moving house and want to get rid of all the junk they've accumulated over the years. The next thing they know, the whole neighborhood's thrown *their* junk in, and the Dumpster's full.

We all want to be open-minded. Human knowledge and human understanding are charging along at an ever-increasing pace. New technologies appear all the time. There are fresh ideas popping up in countless other areas, too, from music to books to movies to the internet—everywhere you turn, in other words. If you don't have a flexible mind, if you can't absorb and adapt to all these new ideas, you're in difficulties. At the same time, you don't want your head to become like that Dumpster: full of other people's garbage.

So, how do you strike the balance?

Most of the answer is a natty little device called *critical thinking*.

We'll be talking about critical thinking much more in the chapter called "Building Your Own Bullshitometer" (page 65). A lot of people don't know there's even such a thing as critical thinking (or analytical thinking, as it's sometimes called). As far as they're concerned, we're all born knowing how to think—it's not something we need to learn. And it's easy to understand their mistake: While even the brightest human beings are capable of being quite numbingly stupid, and groups of people can be even stupider than that, overall there's no denying that we're a very intelligent species. But, just in the same way that the world's most powerful computer is only as good as the software you put into it, a human being needs not just to have the *ability* to think but also to know how to do it—something we have to learn.

This isn't such an odd idea as it might at first seem. You wouldn't be understanding these words unless at some point you'd learned to read. There's nothing controversial about saying people are born with enough intelligence to be able to read, but need to learn how to actually do it. Well, it's the same way with thinking. Even so, plenty of folk are resistant to the notion that rational thinking doesn't just come naturally. Try telling someone they don't know how to think and see what happens.

Where does common sense fit into all this? Many people will tell you that all you really need is a healthy share of common sense, and it's true that common sense can be a useful tool. It's common sense that tells us it's a bad idea to play in traffic or jump off high buildings.

The trouble is that common sense can also be extremely misleading—which is why dishonest or misguided people often use false appeals to common sense in order to try to persuade others that their baloney must be the truth. Common sense might tell us it's ridiculous to believe human beings and cockroaches are related, or that the earth's a rapidly spinning sphere—wouldn't we all just fly off into space?—or that time slows down the faster you travel. Yet we know all these things are true.

This isn't to say we should *ignore* common sense—on the contrary, as we've noted, it can often be very useful. But at the same time we have to be constantly on alert in case it's leading us in the wrong direction. Sherlock Holmes pointed at the problem when he famously said:

> Once you eliminate the impossible, whatever remains,
> no matter how improbable, must be the truth.

Common sense is very good at telling us that things are improbable. The trouble is that it's *too* good at it. It's like a little kid who thinks their cough medicine must be poisonous because it tastes disgusting. Of course, plenty of things that taste disgusting really *are* poisonous, so common sense isn't being entirely foolish here. What it needs is the controlling hand of critical thinking to modify that first, rapid judgement.

⊘

We live in a world that often seems awash with false and/or useless information. We have to remember, too, that it's a world with far more information in it—information *of all kinds*—than people have had to deal with ever before. A few decades ago, various futurologists[1] and plenty of science fiction writers predicted that information would be the currency of the future; most people either didn't believe them or paid no attention, but most people were wrong.

Where most of the predictors themselves got it wrong was in their failure to appreciate fully the problems this development could cause. A first problem is that there's now more information floating around than any of us can readily cope with. A second problem is an economic one: Most of us, given the choice between information we can get for free and information that we have to pay for, will choose the free stuff. This leads to problems three and four.

Problem three is that gathering good information costs money. As a result of people choosing free information sources, most newspapers and TV news channels have had to cut back drastically on their newsgathering staff. And that's just one example. So, even if you're *paying* for information, the quality of the information you're getting is, for straightforward economic reasons, likely to be less good than it should be.

Allied to this is problem four. People who have agendas are only too happy to give you free "information" in hopes of persuading you to their way of thinking. Some of these people are perfectly sincere: They genuinely believe the earth is flat or that NASA faked the moon landings. Others are dishonest. If someone tells you there's no evidence that manmade carbon dioxide emissions are causing climate change, they're either in the pay of the fossil fuels industry or they've been deceived by

---

1. People who get paid to speculate about what, based on current trends, the future might hold.

someone who is—or, conceivably, they've deceived themselves because they can't accept that their pride and joy, that gas-guzzling tank in the driveway, is a big part of the impending catastrophe.

Whatever the source of bad information, whatever the reason someone has for trying to foist it upon you, it can often be hard to tell it from the real thing—and that's where this book comes in. Part One surveys the bullshitosphere and shows how we can adopt some ways of thinking that make it much easier for us to distinguish bad information from good and to demolish the sillier arguments that people use to try to make you believe bullshit. Part Two looks at some of the major areas of bullshit that are poisoning our world and demonstrates how the bogus claims fall apart when subjected to the kind of critical thinking described in Part One.

What I hope *both* parts of the book will do is show you how much *fun* critical thinking can be. Debunking falsehoods isn't just useful in our lives, it can also be a great recreation—like solving puzzles or winning games.

Back at that library meeting, when Franklin used the word "bullshit" I was startled. Not just because, when I was his age, we didn't use words like that around our parents (*his* parents, sitting beside him, obviously thought it was fine!), but also because it seemed to me to be exactly the correct word to use in the context. It was far more direct and accurate than the usual polite terms like "misinformation" and "different perspective." It cut to the core.

I decided, while writing this book, to adopt the word "bullshit" as my standard shorthand for the whole sea of false information (including also deceptive spin, dishonest interpretation, misinterpreted history, conspiracy theories, quack medicine, airheaded woo, pseudoscience, and patent untruth) that has unfortunately come to play such a large part in our daily lives. For a while I even thought the book should be called *The Young Person's Guide to Bullshit*, but I was dissuaded by my editor!

One of the bits of bullshit that has become particularly pernicious is that matters of straightforward reality are somehow regarded as no longer true or false; instead, they are supposedly open to different interpretations depending upon your political worldview. In this book I've tried to steer as clear of politics as possible, but I'm sure some readers are going to think that parts of the text are particularly hard on conservatives or particularly hard on liberals. That isn't the intention.

Reality isn't political. Viruses and distant galaxies and the mechanics of planetary formation—to name just a few—really don't care if you're a liberal or a conservative. The universe keeps on going exactly the same way regardless of how we'd prefer things to be. It isn't a "conservative" attitude to say that the world is just 6,000 years old or to pretend that there isn't overwhelming evidence for evolution; it's just a stupid one. Likewise, it isn't a "liberal" attitude to claim that, despite all the evidence, vaccination causes autism or that homeopathy is better than scientific medicine; it's just a stupid one. And, in the highly unlikely event that the essentials of our understanding of basic scientific issues like these should change, they're going to do so for *scientific* reasons, not political ones.

$$\bigcirc\!\!\!\!\diagup$$

Let me tell you another story. In 1998 the prestigious *Journal of the American Medical Association* published a paper called "A Close Look at Therapeutic Touch." Therapeutic touch is the quack therapy that claims people can be cured of their ills through having their body's invisible energy field manipulated. The touch therapist doesn't actually touch the patient; all that gets touched is this supposed Human Energy Field (HEF). Orthodox science has been unable to detect the HEF, but therapeutic touchers not only know it's there, they know enough about it to be able to mold it into desirable configurations.

Yeah, right.

The experimenter behind this scientific paper, Emily Rosa, thought this was likely all bullshit. To test the therapists' claims, she constructed a setup whereby the therapists pushed their hands through a hole in a screen. On the far side of the screen, invisible to them, a volunteer held out an upturned palm beneath the therapists' hands. The task for the therapists was to identify from the HEF whether it was a right or a left palm that was being offered. Rosa persuaded a number of touch therapists to take part, all of whom presumably assumed they'd pass her test with flying colors. In fact, the result across all of her trials was that the therapists got the right answer about 50 percent of the time—exactly what you'd expect from mere chance.

What's especially interesting about the experiment—aside from the fact that it effectively demolished any claims therapeutic touch might have had to scientific respectability—was that it was devised by Emily for her school science fair; she was nine years old at the time. Her mother and stepfather, Linda Rosa and Larry Sarner, helped her write up her results, as did psychiatrist Dr. Stephen Barrett, a renowned debunker of quackery. (His website *Quackwatch* is required reading for any student of debunking.) Dr. Barrett also helped Emily and her family set up a repetition of the experiment under more controlled circumstances, so there could be no doubt as to the validity of the results. At the time, Emily was the youngest researcher ever to publish a paper in a recognized, peer-reviewed scientific journal. Her record wasn't surpassed until 2010, when at least some of the twenty-five contributors to a study of bees published in *Biology Letters* were just eight years old.

The point is that there's no lower age limit governing the ability to detect bullshit. Emily Rosa's experiment more or less consigned therapeutic touch to the Dumpster of history.

⊘

. . . One final question: How certain am I that none of my *own* ideas are bullshit?

Well, I've tried my best. I'm pretty confident I've eliminated all the examples of my own wrongheadedness that threatened to sneak into this book, and there have been other people reading the text besides me. Even so, we're all susceptible to silly ideas, no matter how much we think we aren't—in fact, the surer we are that we get *everything* right, the more likely it is we've got something wrong.

Humility is a pretty important characteristic to cultivate, too.

⊘

PART ONE

———————

FACING UP TO MISINFORMATION

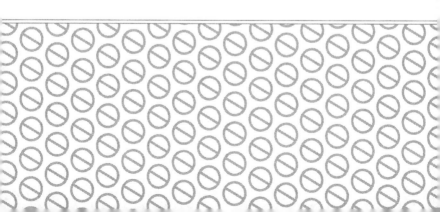

1. THIS STUFF IS EVERYWHERE

So the first and most obvious question, when it comes to misinformation, is why it's so pervasive. If it's wrong, how can so many believe it? And why do people spread so much bogus information? You can hardly spend ten minutes on the internet without discovering all sorts of bullshit, from people claiming that smoking isn't harmful to others who say you can cure cancer by taking their (usually expensive) dietary supplements, and yet others who believe that AIDS was invented by the CIA.

Most of the people spouting online bullshit sincerely believe that what they're saying is true. They may have been lied to by someone and believed the lies because they seemed logical. They may have an ideology (political or religious) that makes them cling to falsehoods despite all the evidence to the contrary. Or they may believe something untrue because all the people around them believe it—or claim to believe it—and they don't want to be the odd one out.

A good example of these factors all working together is the "debate" over manmade climate change—also known as anthropogenic global warming (AGW). We'll go into more detail about climate change later (see page 183), but I'll just briefly touch on it here. The reason I put the word "debate" in quotation marks is that, scientifically, there's really no disputing the evidence. That climate change is happening, and that it's due to human activities, has been shown to be true beyond all sensible doubt.

Unfortunately for the oil companies, the burning of oil and coal produces most of the so-called *greenhouse gases* that cause global warming (see page 189). It's important that we cut down on these fossil fuels—and fast. But doing so would bite into the oil companies' profits.

To protect their financial interests in the use of fossil fuels, corporations like Exxon and Koch Industries began spreading the lie that there was some doubt about the science involved in climate change. They found a few scientists who were prepared to say they disagreed with the consensus on global warming, either for a fee or because they were among the tiny minority who genuinely *did* disagree with their colleagues' conclusions.[1] The oil companies learned this trick from tobacco companies, which a few decades earlier had persuaded the public there was uncertainty within the medical community about whether or not cigarettes were bad for you. The trick worked all over again. You can find plenty of sincere, intelligent citizens who genuinely believe that the science of climate change is still up for debate.

Believing that climate change is debatable is one thing, but some people started to think it was important to take a *political* stance on the issue. Of course, politics can have all sorts of effects on how science is conducted—usually through funding or not funding it—but it has absolutely no power over the laws of nature. If the laws of nature dictate that burning fossil fuels is warming the atmosphere to dangerous levels, it makes no difference whether we're conservatives or progressives—the atmosphere keeps getting warmer no matter what we think. Yet people

---

1. Science doesn't deal in proofs, the way math does. It deals in explanations, called *theories*. By the time something becomes a theory it has been tested and re-tested thousands of times. It's very rare for a theory to be completely overturned. Even so, every theory has its genuine scientific dissidents, some of whom are just nuts but some of whom may not be.

seemed to make that false connection, and, for political reasons, started to spread the idea all over the web that the science was dubious, or even a hoax.

Once again, we should be clear about this: It's not "conservative" to believe in conspiracy theories about climate change being a hoax any more than it's "liberal" to believe that vaccination causes autism. Neither belief has anything to do with politics. In both cases, their position on the political spectrum is neither right nor left but the spot marked "false."

DO PEOPLE REALLY BELIEVE THIS BULLSHIT?

The answer is, depressingly, yes. Every now and then surveys appear showing what people believe about important issues, usually scientific ones, and the results are almost always dismaying.

Only about half of the adults in the US know that the earth travels around the sun, according to a 2000 survey by the National Science Board, and about one in five US adults thinks our pattern of days and nights arises because the sun goes around the earth daily, not because the earth is spinning.

A 2010 Gallup poll of US adults found that they ranked climate change as the least worrying of eight environmental concerns. Also in 2010, a poll done by the University of Texas and the *Texas Tribune* newspaper found that only about one-third of Texas adults knew that humans evolved from earlier species. The list of such poll results could go on indefinitely, but you can see the gloomy picture they paint.

Fortunately (or unfortunately, depending on how you look at it), we aren't the only country that believes the bullshit. A 2011 Russian survey by the state pollster VsTIOM showed that 29 percent of Russians think humans and dinosaurs coexisted, 55 percent believe there's no such thing as natural radioactivity—it's all manmade—and 32 percent think the Earth is at the center of the solar system.

And it's not just in the sciences that we're ignorant. In late 2013 in the UK, a ComRes poll done for the Christian Institute offered people a list of items relating to the stories of Christ's birth and asked them to identify the ones that were actually in the Bible. The results were sometimes embarrassing. About 5 percent of the people surveyed thought that Santa Claus was featured in the Biblical accounts, and about 7 percent thought a Christmas tree was present at the Nativity. In both instances, those percentages roughly doubled among younger adults.

In the United States, the Barna Research Group does similar surveys about people's knowledge of the Bible. Again, some of the results are startling. About 38 percent of American adults think the whole Bible, including the Old Testament, was written after Jesus's death; three-quarters think that the phrase "God helps those who help themselves" comes from the Bible (it doesn't); 16 percent think the *Book of Thomas* is in the Bible (it's in fact in the Apocrypha); and—my favorite!—12 percent think Joan of Arc was Noah's wife.

Although we joke about flat-earthers, there are still a few of them around in the supposedly developed nations, the US included. There are far more people who're dedicated to proving that the earth does not go around the sun. In November 2010, there was a conference in Indiana called "Galileo Was Wrong: The Church Was Right: First Annual Catholic Conference on Geocentrism."

I have no idea if there was ever a *Second* Annual Catholic Conference on Geocentrism!

BUT IF *I* SAY IT, IT'S RIGHT—RIGHT?

There's one person who's better equipped than anyone else to make you believe pure, unadulterated bullshit. It's instinctual for you to accept anything this person tells you, and you can get pretty angry if someone else tells you this person's a bullshitter.

This person, of course, is *you*.

Once we get a wrong idea firmly fixed in our heads, it can be very hard to shake it out again. The process of *unlearning* bad information and false knowledge is difficult and sometimes painful. Like kids who refuse to give up believing in the Tooth Fairy, we tend to hang on to our own false conclusions with grim determination.

To see how strong this effect can be, just look at some of the popular conspiracy theories people believe. Conspiracy theorists can become so obsessed that they spend years and huge amounts of money trying to prove their pet theory even after they've been shown conclusive evidence that it's untrue. A prime example of this concerns the birthplace of President Obama.

Barack Obama was born in Hawaii on August 4, 1961. The idea that he might have been born anywhere else seems to have started as a dirty-tricks rumor spread by some of fellow Democratic presidential hopeful Hilary Clinton's supporters during the 2008 primaries. Once Obama had won the primaries, the notion was picked up by various Republican operatives, some of whom claimed he was born in Kenya, the country where his father was born. If Barack Obama wasn't born in the US, the argument went, he was ineligible to be US president.[1]

On June 12, 2008, President Obama released his official "short form" birth certificate, which showed he was born in Hawaii. This should have settled the question once and for all.

It didn't.

On April 27, 2011 the White House released certified copies of President Obama's original Certificate of Live Birth (his "long form" birth certificate). This, too, showed he was born in Hawaii.

All this time, Barack Obama's original birth announcements, published back in 1961 in the *Honolulu Advertiser* and the *Honolulu Star–Bulletin*, had been available to anyone who cared to go through the archives of either newspaper. The *Honolulu Advertiser* even put a photograph of its original 1961 announcement up on its website to show that the record was accurate and available.

Despite all the extant information, a May 2011 Gallup poll indicated that 13 percent of adult Americans still thought President Obama wasn't born in Hawaii.

The people who believed this conspiracy theory—the Birthers, as they came to be known—believed that their *fake* version of history was somehow *more real* than the reality. Initially they may have been fed the false information by seemingly reliable sources, including talk-radio hosts or prominent Birthers like the California dentist/attorney, Orly Taitz. If this false information intrigued them, some basic inter-

---

1. His opponent in the 2008 presidential race, John McCain, was born in Panama. Just, y'know, sayin'.

net searching could turn up scraps of information that they thought confirmed their suspicions about the president being born in Kenya. Meanwhile, they ignored the mountains of information—including those two birth certificates—that showed he was born in Hawaii and was a bona fide US citizen.[1]

To put it another way, they believed their own bullshit.

THE DUNNING–KRUGER EFFECT

In 1999, two Cornell University psychologists, Justin Kruger and David Dunning, published a paper called "Unskilled and Unaware of It: How Difficulties in Recognizing One's Own Incompetence Lead to Inflated Self-Assessments." Their paper argued that

> . . . when people are incompetent in the strategies they adopt to achieve success and satisfaction, they suffer a dual burden: Not only do they reach erroneous conclusions and make unfortunate choices, but their incompetence robs them of the ability to realize it.

In other words, not only do ignorant people make errors but their ignorance makes it hard for them to recognize that they've done so. The two psychologists investigated further, finding that ignorant and "unskilled" people tended to greatly overestimate their cognitive skills.

---

1. This is an example of a psychological process called confirmation bias—see page 77 for more.

(Knowledgeable and "skilled" people, by contrast, tended to estimate their abilities accurately, or even underestimate them.)

You can see the Dunning–Kruger effect in action on any of the science-denial sites, especially in the comments, whether the subject be climate change or evolution, vaccination or quack medicine. The writers offer "theories" and criticisms that occasionally seem quite convincing at first glance but fall apart quickly under closer inspection. It doesn't seem to occur to the writers that there's a very obvious reason why professional scientists who've spent years studying the subject are ignoring these points! The writers know far less than they think they know, and they're too ignorant of the subject to realize just how much they don't know.

It isn't just random commenters who can become the victims of their own ignorance. Scientists themselves can fall into the Dunning–Kruger trap. Often you'll find chemists or neurosurgeons disputing climate science or geology, claiming that their expertise in another scientific field qualifies them to comment on all science-related matters. In fact, neurosurgeons are very little better equipped to deal with the enormously complicated subject of climate science than the rest of us. Someone skilled in one branch of science can be a complete ignoramus in another.

Consider this: How happy would you be about having a climate scientist stick a scalpel into your brain?

If everyone from conspiracy theorists to highly educated scientists can fall victim to the Dunning–Kruger effect, so can you. The next time your own little bullshit-emitter starts telling you that astrophysicists or historians have been getting it All Wrong, take a second to remember the Dunning–Kruger effect and that the most dangerous bullshitter of all can be yourself.

AUTHORITY FIGURES
AND THE ABUSE OF POWER

In September 2011, the presidential primaries were in full swing. One of the candidates was the Republican Jon Huntsman, who made it very plain that he thought his party could find itself in great danger if it habitually rejected established science. On August 18, 2011, he tweeted:

> To be clear. I believe in evolution and trust scientists on global warming. Call me crazy.

This tweet, combined with Huntsman's other statements about global warming, enraged conservative talk-radio host Rush Limbaugh, who began declaring that Huntsman had betrayed conservatism by espousing these "radical" positions. On September 8, 2011, Limbaugh said:

> You got this guy Huntsman out there spreading a bunch of garbage that 98 percent of all scientists agree that manmade global warming is taking place? It's a hoax! It's bogus.

Of course, leaving aside the merits of the science, Huntsman had been telling the undisputable truth when he said that 98 percent of climate scientists (not "all scientists," as Limbaugh misquoted him[1]) agreed about global warming. In addition to misquoting Jon Huntsman, Limbaugh's dramatic, "It's a hoax! It's bogus." claim is Grade A

---

1. A straw man subterfuge—see page 53.

Bullshit—it's a statement made by someone entirely unqualified in the relevant science and is based on zero evidence.

Nevertheless, Limbaugh, with his huge and devoted radio audience, is an enormously influential figure in US conservative politics. Although Huntsman refused to be cowed by Limbaugh's onslaught, some of his fellow Republican candidates hurried to publicly reassure the broadcaster that they, too, rejected climate science and believed the conspiracy theory that global warming is just a hoax.

To lots of Limbaugh's listeners and to countless others who learned of the fracas elsewhere, this represented confirmation that the rising levels of greenhouse gases in the atmosphere were nothing to worry about. They'd been reassured by people they regarded as authority figures—the famous broadcaster and the politicians.

It's almost impossible to tell whether Limbaugh and the politicians actually believed what they were saying about climate change. Most likely, they were hoping to personally benefit by telling a gullible section of the public what it wanted to hear. If so, that was an enormous abuse of power by the misinformers.

The blame doesn't just rest on Limbaugh and the climate change–denying politicians, however. This situation was also a failure on the part of those who allowed themselves to be persuaded that climate change was nothing to worry about. To accept broadcasters and politicians as authority figures on scientific subjects is, well, pretty stupid.

OKAY, THERE'S A WORLD OF BS OUT THERE, BUT DOES IT REALLY MATTER?

Well, yes, it does. If you're really asking this question, it sounds like you need to read the next chapter . . .

🚫

2. THE DAMAGE THAT IT DOES

Bullshitting is not a victimless crime.

In January 2009 two-year-old Kent Schaible developed symptoms including sore throat, congested lungs, and diarrhea. His parents, Herbert and Catherine Schaible, were members of Philadelphia's First Century Gospel Church, whose Reverend, Nelson Ambrose Clark, maintains that "Our teaching is to trust Almighty God for everything in life: for health, for healing, for protection, for provisions, for avenging of wrongs." Accordingly, Herbert and Catherine didn't take Kent to a doctor. Instead, they prayed over him. It took him ten days to die of what turned out to have been bacterial pneumonia—a serious but perfectly curable condition.

Although the Assistant Medical Examiner of Philadelphia decreed that the death was a homicide, the parents were charged not with murder but with involuntary manslaughter. At trial, they claimed they hadn't realized how seriously ill their son was, and they were sentenced to probation—with instructions to provide proper medical care for their remaining children should any fall ill.

In April 2013 history repeated itself, and the Schaibles' eight-month-old son Brandon died of untreated bacterial pneumonia, dehydration, and group B streptococcus infection. This time the parents were convicted of third-degree murder and sentenced to up to seven years in jail. In a sense they were unlucky that they'd killed the two children in Pennsylvania. Had they lived in Arkansas, Idaho, Indiana,

Iowa, Kansas, Louisiana, Minnesota, New Jersey, Ohio, Oklahoma, Oregon, Rhode Island, Tennessee, Texas, Utah, Virginia, Washington, West Virginia, or Wisconsin, the plea would have been allowable in court that they were merely exercising their religious freedom.

The First Century Gospel Church has run into trouble in this context before. In 1991 nearly 500 children of that church and the nearby Faith Tabernacle Congregation contracted measles because of ideologically motivated failure to vaccinate, and six of those children died.

In sentencing the Schaibles, Judge Benjamin Lerner told them: "You've killed two of your children—not God, not your church, not religious devotion: you." It wasn't their religious faith that led them to kill their children. It was the fact that they believed, and acted upon, bullshit fed to them by people claiming religious authority.

Unfortunately, the Schaibles are far from alone in having killed their children for such reasons. As long ago as 1983 there had already been so many similar cases that the organization Children's Healthcare is a Legal Duty (CHILD) was set up to try to do something about it. If you go to CHILD's website[1] you'll find case after heartrending case of children killed by parents who fell for bullshit.

It's not just misguided prayer, of course. In one recent instance, in 2013, seven-year-old Ryan Alexander Lovett of Calgary, Ontario, died from a strep infection. His mother, rather than take him to a doctor, had insisted on treating him solely with homeopathic medicines, and after his death she was charged with criminal negligence. Ryan's disease could easily have been cured with antibiotics.

---

1. http://childrenshealthcare.org/.

Apologists for medical bullshit often point out that their particular quackery is in itself harmless. Prayer doesn't kill people. Homeopathic medicines, which are just water, don't poison people. If you drink lots of orange juice to treat your cancer, the worst harm you're likely to do is give yourself a bad dose of the runs. So long as the needles have been properly sterilized, acupuncture won't harm you. And so on.

All of this is perfectly true, but it ignores one very obvious fact.

The reason the two Schaible children died was that they got the prayer *instead of* the medical attention. Quack cancer cures kill people because the sufferers don't go see a real doctor until it's too late. Failing to be vaccinated doesn't hurt you, but if you catch measles or polio or small pox, then you'll suffer harm because you didn't get vaccinated. (I've devoted a whole chapter to the antivaxers and the harm they've caused—see page 161.)

The comedian Peter Sellers—the original Inspector Clouseau in the *Pink Panther* movies—died in 1980. He had suffered heart problems for years, following a heart attack in 1964. Frightened of the bypass operation his doctors recommended, he instead started consulting "psychic surgeons." These quacks claim they use paranormal powers to perform surgery without anesthetics, pain, or scarring. In fact, what they use are sleight-of-hand tricks to convince patients and spectators that surgery has been accomplished when it actually hasn't. By the time Peter Sellers's friends were able to convince him his life depended on real rather than psychic surgery, it was too late. Moreover, his ill health had given him years of misery. The psychic surgery killed him not through doing him direct harm but through persuading him he could avoid the medical treatment he so much needed.

THE GREAT AIDS TRAGEDY

AIDS (Acquired Immunodeficiency Syndrome) is a lethal medical condition brought about through infection by a virus called HIV (for Human Immunodeficiency Virus). It's a disease of the immune system: What kills sufferers is not the disease directly but those diseases which their immune system can no longer cope with. Transmission of HIV from one person to another is via the sharing of bodily fluids, especially blood, as can happen during unprotected sex, through blood transfusion, and if drug users share needles. Although there's as yet no cure, there have been great strides in treatment, primarily using the so-called antiretroviral drugs, so that some people infected with the virus can expect to live a full lifespan.

Various strategies have been used in attempts to reduce the rates of AIDS infections. Most countries now have stricter controls over the blood used for transfusions than ever before. Major campaigns are underway in many countries to promote the use of condoms, usually through making sure they're easily available and either cheap or free. Similarly, especially in major cities, many countries have introduced needle-exchange programs, whereby addicts can, with no questions asked, hand in used syringes and receive sterile ones in return.

All of these efforts at prevention have been hindered in one way or another by the merchants of bullshit.

First there have been the moralizers, those who for religious or other reasons object to the ready availability of condoms or safe syringes. They argue that the safest form of sex is abstinence—that the availability of birth control encourages promiscuity—and that drug addicts should just quit.

Both of these arguments look great on paper but make no sense in situations where you're dealing with real human beings. Abstinence-only sex education has been demonstrated by various clinical researches to be counterproductive in preventing unwanted pregnancies and the transmission of disease—essentially because the resolve of even the most dedicated abstainers may crack, and when it does they almost certainly won't have any contraceptives available. Talking about a study she'd co-authored in 2011, Kathrin F. Stanger-Hall of the University of Georgia summarized (my italics): "Our analysis adds to the *overwhelming evidence* indicating that abstinence-only education does not reduce teen pregnancy rates."

A further point worth noting is that, if one partner in a relationship cheats on the other, the innocent person may suffer for the other's unsafe sex.

Also obstructing the effort to curb AIDS was for a long time the myth that the disease is a "gay plague"—that it affects only male homosexuals. Sexually active male homosexuals are indeed the people most at risk, but the disease has claimed countless heterosexual victims. It was perhaps because of the "gay plague" stupidity that Ronald Reagan, the president during whose administration the disease really began to take hold in the western world, including the US, failed even to mention this rapidly escalating public health crisis until September 1985, when he'd been nearly five years in office. It wasn't until May 1987 that he admitted publicly that there was an epidemic underway and set the wheels in motion to do anything about it. By then there were 30,000 diagnosed cases of AIDS in the US, with perhaps several times that many HIV infections. It's obviously difficult to put a number to the avoidable deaths resulting from the delay in taking action, but it can't have been small—just alerting people to the crisis might have saved numerous lives.

An urban myth has made heavy inroads that HIV is a manmade virus that the CIA is using either to control or exterminate black people. Another alarmingly prevalent conspiracy theory is that people who take new AIDS drugs are being used as guinea pigs by the government; because of this myth, people have refused the drugs that might have saved them.

There have been reports of people believing that HIV and AIDS don't exist—that the real killers are the antiretroviral drugs forced upon patients—or that people are safe enough so long as they have a good shower after sex. And, of course, the usual battalions of vitamin-peddlers and bogus "nutritionists" have been on hand to say that scientific medicine can't treat AIDS: The only hope is their quack remedy.

In 2003 there were reports that the Indian government was backing cow urine as a cure for a whole spectrum of diseases, AIDS included. In January 2007 Yahya Jammeh, President of the Gambia, announced that he'd had a dream in which his ancestors had told him AIDS wasn't a viral disease, whatever scientific medicine said, and revealed to him a herbal nostrum that would cure AIDS within three to ten days. In the UK the popular "nutritional therapist" Patrick Holford recommended vitamin therapies, while his compatriot, the climate change denialist Christopher Monckton, announced in November 2009 that he was "working on a cure for infections including HIV"—a cure that has yet to be revealed.

By far the worst single instance of bullshit about AIDS was that of the Thabo Mbeki administration in South Africa. Mbeki was persuaded by opportunist quacks and AIDS denialists that AIDS was a non-viral disease that could be treated with massive doses of vitamins or other "natural" therapies; he flirted, too, with the conspiracy theory that AIDS was invented by the CIA as part of its plot to . . . well, identifying the purpose of the CIA's plot has always been a difficulty with this particular conspiracy theory.

The precise death toll in South Africa consequent upon the efforts of Mbeki and his health minister, Manto Tshabalala-Msimang, to quash the treatment of AIDS patients with modern medicine will probably never be known, but it is certainly of a scale that would justify the use of the word "holocaust." In 1990 there were almost zero HIV cases in South Africa; by 2004 about one person in three was infected. South Africa's Medical Research Council estimated that the years 2005–2006 saw 336,000 South Africans die of AIDS—a truly horrific figure.

"REPRESSED MEMORY SYNDROME"

For too many years, social workers investigating cases of suspected child sexual abuse believed the following mantra, as did the legal system that relied on the evidence of those "experts":

- Always believe children who say they've been sexually abused— they're invariably telling the truth.
- If children say they *haven't* been sexually abused even though the social worker suspects they might have been, they're lying through terror of the abuser. The more they refuse to say they've been abused, the more terrified they are and the worse their suffering must have been.

A third part of the mantra ran like this:

- However, a skilled, empathetic interrogator—such as the social worker currently giving evidence to you—can get the truth out of these recalcitrant children.

So the idea was that the children were invariably telling the truth if they agreed with the person interviewing them, but lying if they *dis*agreed with the person interviewing them. This was the same principle as the one used by the torturers of the Spanish Inquisition—or indeed by "enhanced interrogators" throughout history: The truth is what the torturer has already decided it is, and the torture will go on until the victim says what the torturer demands, whether that's truth or complete bullshit.

In the instance of the social workers and the supposedly sexually abused children, however, there was a further complicating factor:

Small children lie.

They can lie because they're seeking the approval of the adult who's asking them questions, or they can lie just for the fun of it, or they can tell untruths (which is slightly different from flat-out lying) due to a general confusion in their memory of events or because they have difficulty distinguishing truth from fantasy. Exploring the psychological background would take far more space than we have here, but even if we did so we'd find ourselves back at the same place:

Small children lie.

One extra point. Any halfway-trained, halfway-intelligent, halfway-conscientious social worker, child welfare officer, or district attorney should be perfectly aware of this. That didn't stop numerous of these supposed professionals from bringing people to court on serious charges of sexual abuse based on evidence that was often no more than an unsubstantiated accusation coaxed out of an infant, without the remotest circumstantial backup. Sometimes the tales told by the children were so farcical as to be impossible for any sane human being to believe.

Take the case of school bus driver Robert Halsey, convicted in 1993 of repeatedly sodomizing two young twins on their way to and from school. None of the other bus passengers noticed anything. The boys were never late to school nor late home, so when could the crimes have taken place? Sometimes, the court heard, Halsey would force the boys to watch him catch a few fish, which he might stick up their rear ends. This is one you definitely should not try at home! The kids obviously hadn't ever checked out a freshly caught fish.

And they didn't make their accusations until a year and a half later, just after their mother had given birth to a new baby. One further widely known reason young children to lie is to jealous attention-seeking.

Yet not only was Halsey jailed, his several appeals have been turned down. This is clearly a case of the legal profession believing that the maintenance of its dignity—or some such bullshit—is more important than a man's life.

Unfortunately, Halsey's case is far from isolated. Although many similar verdicts have been reversed on appeal, people have lost years of their lives and sometimes much more. And there are plenty of instances of people still rotting in jail, their appeals, like Halsey's, refused, on the grounds of evidence that is either nonexistent or beyond all credibility.

Complicating matters was the pseudoscientific notion of Repressed Memory Syndrome.[1] Although never much accepted by professional psychologists, the idea was widely embraced by social workers and by a few in the psychiatric profession. It was believed that people—specifically, young children—would suppress the memories of traumatic experiences to shield themselves from the pain of those memories. The memories didn't go away, however, and the continued suppression of them could have damaging psychological effects. However, a skilled, empathetic interrogator—now, where have we heard that phrase before?—could tease the memories back out into the open. Confronting those memories would allow the person to begin the healing process . . . and would also, with luck, allow the avid social worker to get someone prosecuted!

All through the 1980s and 1990s there were high-profile cases in which whole communities of parents were charged with child sexual abuse on a massive scale. At about this same time there was a hysteria going on about Satanic cults, which were apparently infesting suburbia everywhere. Inevitably, the two hysterias were conflated, so that now the abuse was often occurring as part of a Satanic ritual.

Eventually sense prevailed, and in case after case it was demonstrated that the supposed crimes had in reality been invented by the social workers, who had used sophisticated means of persuading gullible children to "remember" events that had never in fact taken place. The social workers in most instances probably didn't even realize they'd invented the crimes; they probably thought they were merely "confirming their suspicions."

---

1. Sometimes called Recovered Memory Syndrome, and now more often called False Memory Syndrome.

Even so, it's difficult to comprehend why at least some of them didn't think to stand back, look at what they were claiming as reality, and say, "This is beyond belief!"—and why prosecutors, judges, and jurors so rarely did the same.

Again, innocent people served jail sentences, families were destroyed, and some people are still rotting in prison because of legal officers who're reluctant to admit that sometimes their profession can believe bullshit.

"SAFE" SMOKING

It was in the 1930s that the link between smoking and lung cancer was first established. Unfortunately, this happened in Germany. The Nazis, whose scientific record was in most areas appalling,[1] were surprisingly sound on public health. They mounted various anti-smoking campaigns. When World War II ended, however, their work in this area was initially discarded along with the rest of the junk "Nazi science." (At the same time, of course, the victorious Allies were busily recruiting Nazi rocket scientists. The Nazis were good at rocket science, too!)

A few years later, in the early 1950s, the science about smoking was rediscovered in the US and the tobacco companies wondered how they could minimize the consequent damage to their profits. They realized the public wouldn't respond well to a straightforward ad campaign saying the medical researchers had gotten it All Wrong and smoking

---

1. For example, they rejected evolution, believed in an Aryan master race (see page 44), practiced eugenics (see page 109), and trashed "Jew science" like Relativity in favor of a crackpot theory that the universe was made of ice!

was safe. Instead, the companies set up a fake think tank, the Tobacco Industry Research Committee (TIRC), which hired compliant scientists to *cast doubt* on the scientific consensus. So long as the public thought the case against cigarettes wasn't cast-iron, the companies reasoned, people would tend to assume they could ride their luck.

The tactic was hugely successful, and there was a delay of many years before public health officials could finally enforce such steps as putting warnings on cigarette packs. The lesson learned by the tobacco companies—that hiring useful idiots to cast false doubt on scientific research is the way to go—was noted by the fossil fuel companies. Corporations like Exxon and Koch Industries have used exactly the same technique to deceive the public about climate change.

There was a further long struggle over the issue of secondhand smoking, with the cigarette companies' think tanks saying the evidence of its dangers was slight even though it was perfectly obvious the evidence was solid. A few minutes' browsing on the internet will show you there are *still* some people who believe the companies' propaganda.

Today, even though in many countries there are controls over where people are allowed to smoke, the cigarette companies have carried the fight to nations like Australia and to the developing world. When the Labour Government in Australia took action to have graphic warnings printed on cigarette packs, British American Tobacco, Imperial Tobacco, and Philip Morris International spent a huge amount of money attempting to swing the 2010 election. That same year, Philip Morris International sued Uruguay's government over its insistence that health warnings should cover 80 percent of a cigarette pack's surface; the case is still underway. Since the corporation's annual turnover is about twice Uruguay's GDP, this is something of a Goliath-versus-David fight—and an attempt at a gross violation of national sovereignty that other countries might do well to see as a warning.

How many lives have been cut short because of the tobacco companies' bullshit? How many people have had their lives ruined by smoking-related illnesses? How many kids have died because of second-hand smoking? How many men have been rendered sexually impotent through smoking? How many people have had to have limbs amputated because of their smoking habit? And how many children are *right now* being turned on to smoking by the uninhibited marketing campaigns the cigarette companies are running in the developing world?

Estimates differ, but everyone agrees the numbers are huge.

The pretense that the science on the hazards of smoking was dubious was, of course, utmost bullshit from the moment the cigarette companies began their campaign back in the 1950s. It's a bit of bullshit that has killed millions.

THE MASTER RACE

During the eighteenth century it became clear to German thinkers (as it did to their counterparts in other European countries) that the Bible's account of Adam and Eve was probably not literally true. Where, then, had white people—the supposed pinnacle of humanity—come from? Africa was out of the question, of course. It was known that some of the civilizations in Asia were incredibly ancient. Since it wasn't at the time widely appreciated that the earth could be much older than humankind, these very old civilizations of India and China were thought to be almost as old as the world. Naturally, the people who were living in India and China *now* couldn't be the original, pure-blooded human stock, because they weren't white . . .

And so, from several strands of baloney thinking, there arose the anthropological myth of a primordial white race of humanity, the Aryans, who arose in the general region of the Himalayas—for some reason high mountains and a moderate climate were regarded as an important prerequisite for the emergence of topnotch specimens of humanity.[1] Fastidiously avoiding any interbreeding with other races, the Aryans emigrated from India and finally ended up in and around Germany. There, for reasons unexplained, they finally *did* do some interbreeding, but it was with Nordics and so was regarded as strengthening rather than weakening the race.

Even after it had become evident that the planet was hugely older than earlier thought—and that humankind was a relative latecomer to the scene—the pseudoscience concerning the Aryans remained popular among white racists all over Europe and North America. It still hangs around even today, causing human misery wherever its cancer spreads. The fact that the legend has been demonstrated time and time again to be false—that it *cannot possibly* be true—means nothing to the hatemongers.

The place where the Aryan bullshit did the most concentrated damage was, of course, Nazi Germany.

There were all sorts of ways a Nazi could tell you weren't an Aryan. If you were a Jew or a gypsy, or if your skin color wasn't white, that was an obvious giveaway. The Slavic peoples, the Poles, the Serbs—

---

1. Some revisionist thinkers claimed the Aryans originated in the lost continent of Atlantis (see page 244). And why not? There's as much reason to believe in Atlantis as there is in the Aryans.

all were obviously subhuman. Surely no Aryan would be homosexual or mentally handicapped. The list went on. Some "defective" people were merely sterilized and/or incarcerated in concentration camps; as all the world knows except for a few fervent Holocaust deniers (see page 226), millions of others were murdered at random, starved to death, or slaughtered in highly organized extermination campaigns.

The exact number of people the Nazis murdered is uncertain. Most people agree that about six million Jews were slaughtered, many of them children. Probably about a million Romanies died, plus millions of Serbians, Slovenes, Poles, and Russians. Hundreds of thousands of disabled people were murdered, plus many tens of thousands of Freemasons. Thousands of homosexuals, Jehovah's Witnesses, and people of color were put to death. Some estimates put the total death toll of the Holocaust as high as 30 million or more; most put it at about 15–20 million.

And all because of bullshit.

THE MOST DANGEROUS BULLSHIT OF ALL

The death toll from the Nazis' racist nonsense is absolutely horrific—so huge it can be difficult to take it in. Yet it's only a part of the total caused by modern racism, which came into the ascendant at roughly the same time as the start of the full-scale transatlantic slave trade in the early seventeenth century: It is far easier to behave inhumanely to your fellow humans if you can persuade yourself they're not in fact really humans, and ideas of "inferior races" offered the perfect excuse. Even though institutionalized slavery is no longer with us (which is not to say the slave trade has ended, alas), racism of one kind or another obviously still survives in most of the world's communities, and continues to exact its annual tribute of death and human misery.

But all such casualty figures are as nothing compared to the one we're facing should we career at full speed into catastrophic climate change, which is exactly what we appear to be doing thanks to the bullshit being spread by the fossil-fuels corporations, their shills, and their useful idiots. One common smear about climate scientists has it that they're "alarmists"; it's an especially stupid smear because the climate change we're facing is, as we'll see in a later chapter, something that it's impossible to be too alarmed about. We can expect a death toll in the *billions* unless very soon—like, yesterday—we cut the bullshit and start acting like rational adults.

3. ON WEASEL WORDS

There are patterns in the way that bullshitters argue. Just as politicians tend to use "spin"—rhetorical tricks to make the situation sound better than it really is—so do the folks who are intent on bullshitting you.

Some of these bullshitters are really out-and-out liars trying to bamboozle you. Like the politician spinning the situation, they know the truth and they're trying to make sure you don't learn it, or at least that you only learn the version of it that they endorse. However, even those purveyors of bullshit who sincerely believe in what they're telling you use the same patterns of rhetoric as the out-and-out liars. Perhaps they're so convinced of their own version of the truth that they think winning the argument, by fair means or foul, is all that's important. Perhaps they really don't recognize the difference between a logical argument and an attempt to pull the wool over your eyes. Or perhaps they themselves have been deceived by those same rhetorical tricks and don't even realize they're using them.

QUOTE MINING AND CHERRY PICKING

How often have you watched a movie because of the glowing reviews the distributor has quoted, only to find out halfway through the movie that it totally sucks? You know the kind of review quotes I mean:

EDGE-OF-YOUR-SEAT EXCITEMENT!

or

TEARS . . . RAN FREELY DOWN MY FACE AS I WATCHED THIS . . . TRAGIC LOVE STORY!

How would you feel if you tracked down the original reviews and discovered what the reviewers *really* said was:

> With these stars and this budget you'd expect edge-of-your-seat excitement. What a pity that the result's so unremittingly dire . . .

and

> Tears of laughter ran freely down my face as I watched this supposedly tragic love story.

Movie distributors aren't usually quite so blatant as this in their extraction of favorable quotes, but very often you'll find that a review wasn't quite the rave that the extract made it seem. The technique of selective quotation is called *quote mining*. A very famous example of quote mining comes from the Creationist crowd, who make heavy use of the following quote from Charles Darwin's *Origin of Species* (1859):

> To suppose that the eye with all its inimitable contrivances for adjusting the focus to different distances, for admitting different amounts of light, and for the correction of spherical and chromatic aberration, could have

been formed by natural selection, seems, I freely confess, absurd in the highest degree.

Here, the Creationists cry, we find the very Father of Evolution himself saying that natural selection couldn't produce the human eye! What they neglect to mention is that Darwin *went on* to say that though it might be hard for us to imagine the eye emerging through natural selection, just a few moments' thought shows us that it's not as implausible as we might have first believed. Using only the opening part of Darwin's quote implies that he meant something completely different from what he really did.[1]

A striking example of quote mining on a massive scale occurred in 2009 in the so-called Climategate affair. The main server of the UK's University of East Anglia's Climatic Research Unit (one of the world's most important centers for studying climate) was hacked, and thousands of confidential emails that the Unit's researchers had sent to one another were leaked to climate change-denialist websites and journalists . . . who began quote mining them.

Much was made, for example, of the use by Dr. Phil Jones, the unit's chief, of the word "trick" to describe a particular means of presenting statistical information. Surely the word "trick" implies deceit, right?

Well, no, actually. Can you remember when you learned the trick of riding a bicycle without falling off?

---

1. "Yet reason tells me, that if numerous gradations from a perfect and complex eye to one very imperfect and simple, each grade being useful to its possessor, can be shown to exist; if further, the eye does vary ever so slightly, and the variations be inherited, which is certainly the case; and if any variation or modification in the organ be ever useful to an animal under changing conditions of life, then the difficulty of believing that a perfect and complex eye could be formed by natural selection, though insuperable by our imagination, can hardly be considered real."

No fewer than eight independent investigations of the Climate Research Unit have found there was no misconduct among its scientists, yet still the mined quotes keep being publicized by climate change denialists.

Similar to quote mining is *cherry picking*, which usually deals with data rather than words. For example, when you're sharing your grades with your parents, it's natural to focus on the As first, then the Bs . . . and maybe leave the F in Math until last. If you didn't mention the F at all, and perhaps also failed to bring up that D in Physics, you'd be guilty of cherry picking.

Cherry picking data is a tactic used throughout the bullshitosphere, but perhaps most recognizably by climate change denialists. Graphs of rising atmospheric temperatures don't show a straight line or a nice steady curve; they show a sort of zigzag. The general trend of the zigzag is inexorably upward, but it's easy to find an individual point on the zigzag today that's lower than a point ten years ago. Climate change denialists frequently use exactly this method of cherry picking to claim that the world isn't warming, but is actually cooling down!

Sometimes the cherry picking doesn't involve data but other kinds of evidence. It's a trap that's easy to fall into, even if you're not a bullshitter yourself. We tend to focus on the evidence that supports our beliefs and pay less attention to the evidence that might make us question them. The true bullshitter will ignore the evidence in the latter category or, using one of the tactics described in this chapter, will try to discredit it.

STRAW MEN AND *AD HOMINEM* ATTACKS

Once upon a time some friends of mine were stuck in a line of cars in the Lincoln Tunnel, which links New York City to New Jersey. They got into an argument with the people in another car about who had the right of way. The occupants of both cars opened their windows and started hollering at each other. Finally, my friend Nancy yelled at one of the women in the other car, "And you look stupid in that hat!"

I wasn't there, so I have no idea whether or not the woman *did* look stupid in that hat, but it's pretty obvious that it had nothing to do with whether one car or the other had the right of way. Even so, the remark won the argument.

This incident is a classic example of an *ad hominem* attack. The Latin phrase *ad hominem* means "against the man," meaning that the attack ignores the right or wrong of the argument and instead focuses on an irrelevant supposed failing of the opponent.

In 2009, the climate change denialist Christopher Monckton gave a talk at Bethel University in Minnesota. John Abraham, a professor in Thermal Sciences at the nearby University of St. Thomas, recorded Monckton's lecture and went through it point by point, checking each and every reference Monckton had made to scientific sources, even contacting some of the researchers referenced to make sure he understood their conclusions correctly. Alarmingly, he found that in every instance what Monckton stated the source said differed from what it actually *did* say. In May 2010, Abraham published the results online as an eighty-four-minute audiovisual presentation entitled, "A Scientist Replies to Christopher Monckton," in which he demolished every single one of the "scientific" claims Monckton had made in the lecture.

Monckton was not amused. In one attack he made on Abraham he said:

> . . . so venomously *ad hominem* are Abraham's artful puerilities, delivered in a nasal and irritatingly matey tone (at least we are spared his face—he looks like an overcooked prawn). . .

So here's a challenge for you! Which one of these two was guilty of an *ad hominem* attack?

(a) Abraham, for checking Monckton's claims and finding them false, or
(b) Monckton, for saying that "at least we are spared his face—he looks like an overcooked prawn"?

A *straw man* argument, very often used in politics, is where a person mounts an attack not on an opponent's real beliefs or claims, but on a false version of them. (Quote mining is frequently used in the service of straw man arguments.) For example, if I wanted to mount a straw man attack on Charles Darwin I might say he believed the eye couldn't develop through natural selection and use the mined quote given above as my evidence. Or I could say that his book *Origin of Species* was advancing a racist cause—after all, it even uses the word "races" in its subtitle. In fact, *Origin of Species* deals with evolution in animals and plants, not human beings, and Darwin was using the word "race" in its old sense, meaning "subspecies"! What I'd be doing, then, would be attacking him for a "crime" that I myself had invented . . . but many people wouldn't realize that.

A variant on the straw man argument is false equivalence. A classic false equivalence might be:

- I'm frightened of getting suspended.
- Therefore, I'm frightened of the principal, who could suspend me.
- I'm also frightened of poisonous spiders.
- Therefore, the principal is a poisonous spider.

Depending on the particular principal, this could of course be sort of true! But it's not a logical deduction.

THE GALILEO GAMBIT

"They laughed at Galileo, they laughed at Albert Einstein, they laughed at Alfred Wegener . . ."

The implication is, of course, that, if someone is doubting or laughing at your ideas, they're just showing how right you are, since you're in such good company. The logical fallacy of the *Galileo Gambit* is pretty obvious—after all, they also laughed at Bugs Bunny.

A variation on the Galileo Gambit is the *Gandhi Gambit*. Here's something Gandhi is supposed to have said as part of his advocacy of civil disobedience rather than violence as a means of revolution:

> First they ignore you, then they laugh at you, then they
> fight you . . . then you win.

There's no reliable record of Gandhi ever actually saying this, but it's a good quote anyway. Unfortunately, it's been purloined by bullshitters for use in much the same way as the Galileo Gambit. No matter what your opponent is doing—laughing at you, arguing with you, or just plain ignoring you—this is supposedly merely a stage they're going through on their way to agreeing with you.

THE GISH GALLOP

The creationist Duane Gish developed a style of debate that came to be called the *Gish Gallop*. Gish would insist his opponent go first. After his opponent was finished with his or her argument, Gish would begin talking very quickly for perhaps an hour, reeling off a long string of "facts." His debating opponent, of course, didn't have the chance even to note down all those "facts," let alone work out whether or not they were correct. In his or her rebuttal, the opponent could either ignore Gish's tirade altogether, which would look like dodging the issue, or try to answer as many of the points as possible, which meant looking as if he or she were floundering. Gish's trick was a clever one, and it fooled a lot of audiences.

He didn't always get away with it, however. Several people noticed that Gish's presentation was always the same, right down to the jokes, no matter what his opponent had said. One such opponent was the evolutionary biologist Niall Shanks. Invited to debate Gish, he studied videos of Gish's other debates. Speaking first, Shanks introduced every point he knew Gish was going to make and demolished it.

Vindictively, Shanks also stole all the jokes he knew Gish was going to make.

THE ARGUMENT FROM AUTHORITY

The Gish Gallop is still a popular technique used by bullshitters, and it's sometimes deployed in conjunction with the closely related *argumentum verbosium*, sometimes called the *proof by intimidation*. Here, the bullshitter uses as much obscure information and terminology as possible in making his claim. Perhaps, too, the bullshitter will cite obscure sources or authorities.

The honest reply to this baffling wave of nonsense is that you have absolutely no idea what the bullshitter is talking about . . . except, of course, that this can make you look ignorant and/or stupid in the eyes of the audience—just what the bullshitter wants.

The bullshitter who cites obscure sources as part of the *argumentum verbosium* is relying on the fact that you probably won't bother checking those sources. It's very common for the purveyors of bullshit to write books with huge notes sections at the back, knowing that most people will accept the phony scholarship at face value. In these cases, sometimes someone *does* take on the gargantuan task of checking all the sources, and that can make the bullshitter look pretty silly—we saw what happened when John Abraham checked Christopher Monckton's sources. Most often, though, the people who've been swallowing the bullshit ignore such debunking exercises.

This method of bullshitting assumes that there's nothing wrong with the sources themselves—it's merely that the bullshitter has been misrepresenting them. But what if the "experts" he's citing aren't experts at all? Or perhaps the experts are genuinely experts but, like everyone else, sometimes make mistakes.

Most nonfiction books today use the *argument from authority* extensively. Authors and researchers build on the work of others ("authorities") who've gone before them. The argument from authority can be a very useful tool—imagine how long a modern scientific paper would be if its author were forced to start at the level of the Pythagorean theorem or Euclid's laws and explain every theory or process from the ground up!

Just like the bullshitter who packs the back of his book with a gazillion endnotes referring to dubious sources, the genuine writer cites lots of authorities to back up her claims. Thus the argument from authority can be used either wisely and honestly, or to deceive or mislead. Baloney-mongers very frequently abuse the argument from authority (so much so, in fact, that some people think the term "argument from authority" always implies a dishonest gambit). For example, they may point out that Sir Isaac Newton, one of the greatest physicists of all time, believed that the earth was only a few thousand years old. Who are *you* to disagree with the Great Man?

Well, yes, but when Newton was alive (1642–1727) there was no reason to think the world was anything *but* just a few thousand years old. In 1650 an Irish cleric, Archbishop James Ussher, had carefully counted through the events of the Old Testament and, making lots of assumptions (for example, he simply guessed at the lifespans of quite a lot of the individuals mentioned), had calculated that the earth had been created in 4004 BCE. (He even got specific, stating that the earth was formed during the evening of October 22 of that year!) Ussher was a very widely admired scholar, and his calculations were assumed to be correct. There was no reason for Newton to disagree with them.

There were plenty of other things Newton didn't know. He knew nothing about viruses or bacteria. He didn't know the planets Uranus and Neptune existed, or that the sun's energy comes mainly from the nuclear fusion of hydrogen into helium. He was ignorant of all sorts of bits of knowledge that you and I take for granted. He's a quite useless "authority" to cite in a debate about the age of the earth!

THE PLURAL OF "ANECDOTE" ISN'T "EVIDENCE"

Lots of people believe they've seen UFOs; you may be one of them. The key point is that "UFO" stands for "*unidentified* flying object." I've seen a couple of UFOs myself, one of which I was able to identify within minutes (it was a plane, and the sunlight was catching it at a funny angle) and the other of which took me a bit longer (it was an odd refraction effect). Plenty of people reckon they've seen ghosts, fairies, the Loch Ness monster, and other elusive figures.

To a scientist, all of these anecdotal accounts mean almost nothing in terms of evidence. Just because lots of people have seen unexplained lights in the sky does *not* mean that the earth is being regularly visited by aliens in flying saucers. Some perfectly sincere people have "memories" of being abducted by those same aliens, who subjected them to humiliating physical experimentation. It's worth remembering that a few centuries ago those same lights in the sky were believed to be witches on broomsticks, some of whom could transport people away to force them to take part in, yes, humiliating physical rituals. There's no more reason to believe the anecdotes about flying saucers than there is to believe those about witches.[1]

The professional bullshitter, however, bets on the fact that most of us will think that if lots of people have reported something, then it must be true—or, at least, that the bullshitter's explanation of it must be true.

Of course, it's always possible that the anecdotes really *do* stack up to something that is worth further investigation. But we have to do the actual investigation of the anecdotal evidence, not just assume the collection of anecdotes *is* the investigation.

OTHER CUNNING TRICKS

When President George W. Bush said in 2003 that the science of climate change "isn't settled," it sounded to many people as if he were being admirably cautious. In fact, for years the consensus among climate scientists had been firmly established, and all Bush was doing was using the pretense of caution as an excuse for doing nothing.

The *science isn't settled* trick is far from unique to Bush, though. Some of the people who claim that vaccination is dangerous, when

---

1. It does, though, seem that the people who "remember" their abductions are often perfectly honest: They genuinely believe these things happened to them. There are some good psychological explanations for the phenomenon—many suggesting that hypnagogic dreaming plays a part.

confronted by the overwhelming evidence that it's quite extraordinarily safer than the diseases it protects against, will likewise claim that "the science isn't settled" and point to old and discredited scientific papers that support their beliefs. Related tactics are pointing out false anomalies and shifting the goalposts.

It has often been observed that you need to find just one absolute and incontrovertible proof of a ghost to bring down the idea that there's no such thing as life after death. That single ghost would—or could—represent an anomaly that it'd be hard for the rationalist worldview to explain. A common technique of bullshitters is to extend that argument to include what are, by any sensible definition, *false anomalies*. An annual example of this is when there's a nasty winter blizzard or two. All sorts of people pop up to say that this is "proof" there's no such thing as global warming—all while ignoring the past year's tornadoes, floods, hurricanes or typhoons, droughts, species migrations . . . A single heavy winter snowfall doesn't indicate anything wrong with our scientific understanding of climate change.

The best-known bullshitter use of the tactic known as *shifting the goalposts* concerns transitional fossils. Fossil records offer us snapshots of the life forms that inhabited our planet going back billions of years. Ideally, fossil records would show us a complete picture. However, there are various reasons why they don't:

- Fossils form only in very specific geological circumstances. When a particular plant or animal dies, the odds against its remains undergoing fossilization are enormous.

- If the circumstances are just right, life forms with bones can form fossils relatively easily. But most life forms don't have bones.
- Almost all of the fossils that have ever formed have since been recycled by natural geological processes—they're now rock or soil.
- Fossils that have survived this recycling are usually now in the middle of a sedimentary rock. Since we can't go around busting open every sedimentary rock, we can only ever find just a tiny percentage of all the fossils that exist.

Ignoring all of these points, creationists often demand that biologists should produce fossils of transitional species: If you're saying that chickens are descended from dinosaurs, then where are all the fossils that show creatures midway between *T. rex* and a Rhode Island Red?

In fact, there are lots of intermediate fossils between dinosaurs and modern birds. We can trace all sorts of evolutionary ancestries through the fossil record. Moreover, new fossils are being unearthed all the time. Every now and then—pretty often, in fact—one of those fossils fills in a gap between two previously known prehistoric species. Here's how the routine goes:

- We've just discovered Fossil C, hurray!
- It represents a species that lies halfway between the ones we knew about from Fossil A and Fossil B.

It's at this point that the creationist steps in to complain that we haven't solved the transitional-fossil problem at all, because where are the transitional forms between Fossil A and Fossil C and between Fossil C and Fossil B? It's obvious why this tactic is called shifting the goalposts!

FALSE BALANCE

This isn't a tactic that's primarily annoying because of its use by bull-shitters—although they do use it. *False balance*—or *faux balance*—is often used by news media, whether broadcast, print, or internet, as a lazy way of appearing to give both sides of a story.

In any sphere of human knowledge, you can always find some fruit-bat who disagrees. The earth is round? There's a fruitbat who says it's flat. NASA landed astronauts on the moon? There's a fruitbat who says it was all a hoax mounted by Stanley Kubrick and Arthur C. Clarke. You've had a run of bad luck? There's a fruitbat who says this is just because you haven't been asking the right questions of the universe.[1] And so on.

Most of us can tell that there's a big difference between the rationality of the two viewpoints in each of these arguments. Yet over the past couple of decades or so, more and more of the supposedly objective media outlets have decided that the way to achieve "balance" in their reporting is to put a sane person up against a fruitbat and leave it to an often under-informed audience to sort it out.

---

1. I kid you not. This is exactly the idea put forward in the book and DVD *The Secret* (2006) by Rhonda Byrne and her colleagues—see page 112.

THE "GOD OF THE GAPS" ARGUMENT

Despite the name and the fact that it's often used by religious anti-evolutionists, this fallacy isn't an exclusively religious one. When we're confronted by something we don't understand, most of us try to find a rational explanation. If we don't understand why rainbows happen, for example, we go to Wikipedia and look at the entry on rainbows. There are plenty of people, unfortunately, who refuse to follow that logical course. Instead, they insist that rainbows are magic.

Until just a few years ago, physicists were baffled as to why matter had mass. We all *know* it has mass—drop a brick on your foot and you get immediate proof!—but nobody knew *why*.

Well, some people thought they did. They said this was just one of those things that science couldn't explain: There was a gap, and the only way of filling it was to invoke a supernatural explanation.

As long ago as 1964, various physicists, among them Peter Higgs, said there might be a type of particle—now called the Higgs Boson—that was responsible for this. In 2012, scientists working at CERN finally detected the Higgs Boson. This meant that this particular "god of the gaps" explanation had evaporated. There was no longer a "gap" that science had failed to fill.

In a famous TV interview in 2011, Bill O'Reilly presented an astonishing "god of the gaps" argument to his interviewee, David Silverman. It seems O'Reilly thought the tides, which have been understood by science for centuries as caused by the moon's pull (and partly by the sun's), were actually a proof of God:

I'll tell you why [religion's] not a scam, in my opinion: tide goes in, tide goes out. Never a miscommunication. You [scientists] can't explain that.

Of course, not just rationalists but believers hurried to point out that the tides are pretty well understood and that O'Reilly had made a fool of himself.

Not that O'Reilly agrees with this assessment, of course.

PROJECTION

Finally, there's *projection*, a term that comes from psychoanalysis. In more general usage, it refers to consciously or, more usually, unconsciously ascribing to others your own traits, usually your less desirable ones. So someone who lies and cheats may try to hide this from themselves or others by claiming that *other people* are liars and cheats.

It's a tactic very commonly used by bullshitters. Most obviously, whenever you start trying to persuade a bullshitter to see things rationally, you'll find yourself accused of any or all of the tricks we've looked at in this chapter.

In the next chapter we'll talk about some of the ways you can defend yourself against many kinds of bullshit.

🚫

4. BUILDING YOUR OWN BULLSHITOMETER

As we've said before, there's one person more likely than anyone else to make you believe in bogus information, and it's someone you see every time you look in a mirror. So, when you set out to build a Bullshitometer—a bag of mental tools to help you detect and counter even the most plausible-seeming bullshit—it's a good idea to remember who you're going to be using it against:

Not just everyone else, but YOU.

Of course, as soon as you start using your Bullshitometer you're going to find that sometimes you change your mind on one issue or another. A lot of people think that changing your mind about something is a sign of weakness, or even a lack of integrity. They bray, "Inconsistency!" and use smear-words like "flip-flopping."

One of the most important periods in human history was from the late seventeenth century to the late eighteenth century. It's called the Enlightenment. People in Europe began to re-examine many of the ideas that for centuries they'd taken for granted and discovered that, more often than not, those ideas were false. We've been living in a sort of ideas revolution ever since, and each day we benefit from that. Had it not been for the sea change in human thought that occurred during the Enlightenment, human life would still be nasty, brutish, and short.

We owe a deep debt of gratitude to those people who changed their minds.

Or, as bullshitters would say, who flip-flopped.

Scientists change their minds about things all the time as new information comes along. Only once something has become established as a major theory (see page 67) will they start to regard it as likely true, and even then they'll constantly be investigating its details, with the consensus shifting backward and forward as they get closer and closer (they hope) to the truth.

That's the way intelligent people behave. It's a logical way of going about things, and it very obviously works.

It's not only scientists who operate this way. Successful companies are generally the ones that are ready to adapt the nature of their business in response to change. "If it ain't bust, don't fix it" is a great general rule that a lot of companies wisely subscribe to, but they need to be constantly checking to make sure it *really* ain't bust.

Bullshitters, however, regard "inconsistency" as a failing. This attitude has come to prevail particularly in politics. It can be a death sentence for a politician's career should they change their mind about an issue—should they, in fact, do what smart people do all the time.

But then politics is, let's recall, an arena in which George H. W. Bush could score major political points by claiming he didn't like broccoli.

THE SCIENTIFIC METHOD—THE BASICS

So we've established that it's useful that scientists are constantly revising their opinions. Let's look in a bit more detail at the way scientists approach their quest for the truth.

The Scientific Method is a way of going about the acquisition of knowledge and of understanding the world around us. Despite its name, the approach can often be applied in areas outside the sciences.

The basic form of the Scientific Method dates back to the sixteenth/seventeenth-century English politician and scientist Francis Bacon.[1] To understand a subject, his recommendation was to gather as much information as possible and then try to work out some general principles. Next, test those general principles to see if they offer an explanation. Once you've established several sets of general principles, you can put them together as the basis for your next line of inquiry. This approach is now called *induction.*

In practice, *induction* was useful but hopelessly cumbersome, and almost no one after the seventeenth century actually used it. It was important, though, in that Bacon had recognized the best way to acquire knowledge was via a formal, rigorous approach rather than, for example, believing your hunches or jumping to conclusions.

In the nineteenth century, people formulated a different model, one that's far closer to what we use today. This was *hypothetico-deduction.* In this model, scientists go through the following steps:

- Study the relevant phenomena—gather *evidence.*
- Think of a way in which those phenomena might be explained—form a *hypothesis.*
- Imagine some as-yet-unobserved consequences of the hypothesis—make *predictions* based on the hypothesis.
- Devise *experiments* to find out if these predictions come true.

---

1. Others formulated the idea earlier, notably the tenth/eleventh-century Arab scientist Ibn al-Haytham (Alhazen), but Bacon's formulation was the most influential.

If the predictions are confirmed, the scientists reckon the hypothesis could be correct. For example:

- Studying the night sky, you notice that the stars move across it, so you realize that either the heavens are circling the earth or the earth is spinning—evidence.
- You hypothesize that the earth is spinning—hypothesis.
- After doing some heavy thinking, you predict that, if it's the earth that's spinning, liquids should form a spiral as they flow into relatively narrow apertures—prediction.
- Next time you use the toilet, you test this prediction—and *voila!*—experiment.

The twentieth-century philosopher Karl Popper realized that the hypothetico-deductive method was incomplete because, strictly speaking, that final step didn't mean the hypothesis had actually been confirmed, just that it hadn't been proven false. A complete hypothesis should therefore include not just tests that might confirm it, but also tests that might *falsify* it. In practice this can often be difficult to achieve, so usually scientists are content if many different tests seem to confirm the hypothesis and, even better, if independent lines of inquiry all converge on the same conclusion.

If a hypothesis stands up to all the tests and falsification attempts hurled at it over a good period of time, it achieves the status of a *theory*. Unlike math, science doesn't deal in absolute proofs, because theories are always subject to change or at least modification if better evidence comes along, but a theory that has attracted the support of a large majority of the scientists working in the relevant field[1] is about as near as you can get, in scientific terms, to a proven fact.

This is a much more powerful meaning of the word "theory" than the one we use in general conversation—"I have a theory that Megan Fox is going to win an Oscar." The fact that many people are unfamiliar with the difference between the two meanings is often exploited by bullshitters. How often have you heard Creationists say that the theory of evolution by natural selection is "just a theory"? Matters aren't helped by the fact that scientists themselves often use the word "theory" when really they mean "hypothesis" (String Theory, for example, is actually just a hypothesis so far),—and often, too, they use it in the colloquial sense, just like anyone else.

It's worth looking also at what we mean by the word "prediction" in the description above. One of the most dramatic scientific predictions of all time was made by the UK astronomer Edmond Halley in 1705 when he said the comet that had appeared in 1682 would reappear in 1758. He based this prediction on noticing a pattern among historical records of comets: that there seemed to be a bright one every 76 years. He realized that it must be the same comet reappearing, and, thanks to the theory of gravitation worked out by his friend Isaac Newton, could state with confidence that the object was in orbit around the sun.

It's easy to think that all scientific predictions should be like that: of something that's going to happen in the future. In a sense they are, but the event that's going to happen in the future can be the discovery of something that happened in the past. When Charles Darwin was

---

1. The "in the relevant field" part is important: It's irrelevant whether dentists agree or disagree with an astronomy theory, for example.

working on his theory of evolution he admitted it might be difficult to find transitional fossils—fossils or organisms that lay midway between established species (see page 60). But he predicted that, if his theory was correct, it was possible *some* would be found.

In fact, he was overcautious. *Lots* of transitional fossils have been discovered since Darwin's time. Look up the entry "List of transitional fossils" in Wikipedia and you'll see how long the list is—and, as its authors acknowledge, more could be added![1] The most famous is probably *Archaeopteryx*, a creature that can be seen as midway between the winged dinosaurs and modern birds. Another famous one is *Tiktaalik*, discovered as recently as 2004 and representing the transition from fish to amphibian.

The discovery of all those transitional fossils is a triumphant fulfillment of Darwin's prediction. And it's one of the reasons his theory retains its status as a theory—in other words, as a pillar of human knowledge.

In practice, people often don't follow the steps of the Scientific Method precisely: a step might be missed, or a couple of steps might swap in order. But that's the basic plan.

If we use the Scientific Method in our thinking, we have a powerful analytical tool that'll serve us well when we're confronted by a wide range of problems. Just on its own the Scientific Method is a very good Bullshitometer.

---

1. Creationists and others often sniff that you shouldn't look to Wikipedia for information—as if some Answers in Genesis tract might be more reliable! In fact, for this sort of quick information Wikipedia is usually excellent. I'd double-check the spellings of the species names before using them in a term paper, though . . .

THE SCIENTIFIC PROCESS—THE OTHER STUFF

Science used to be advanced by the efforts of individuals—individuals like Isaac Newton and Marie Curie. But more recently, scientific research has usually been carried out by teams, and the important moment has been not so much the announcement of a team's results as the acceptance of those results by the relevant scientific community at large. This way of advancing by *consensus* may not be so dramatic as individual wild-eyed scientists shouting "Eureka!"—it's not the course Hollywood would have chosen, for sure—but it's very effective.

Very occasionally there'll be a major change in the consensus view. An example came in the late 1950s and early 1960s when the discovery of seafloor spreading led to the development of the theory of plate tectonics. Before then, the geophysics consensus was that the idea the continents could move around, championed by Alfred Wegener and others since the beginning of that century, was impossible. Afterward, the consensus was that the continents could and did "drift." Such a relatively rapid change in the consensus view has been called a *paradigm shift*.

In the practice of professional science today, there are a few other stages that are often described as part of the Scientific Method. In reality, though, they're part of what can be called the scientific *process*. You should be wary of any "great, new scientific breakthrough" that hasn't gone through the following stages, or something like them.

- *Publication* in a scientific journal. There are hundreds, if not thousands, of scientific journals in the world, and a surprising number are disreputable—they're corrupt or phony. Whenever you see that something has been published in a scientific journal and it looks iffy to you, check the journal's entry in Wikipedia to see if it's for real.[1]

- The properly accredited journals use the system of *peer review*. After a paper is submitted, it's sent to other experts in the field (peers) to make sure it's original, useful, and error-free. Only if those experts "okay it" do the journal's editors accept it for publication. This can be a slow and boring process, but it does make it far less likely that erroneous information is published.[2]

- The published papers don't just include what the team concluded from the experiments or research they did. The scientists also *make their raw data available* so that readers can check it for possible error, not only in the data itself but also in the way it was analyzed.

- Finally, details are given so readers can *replicate* the experiments—repeat them to see if they get the same results. If several other teams confirm the results, then they can be accepted as valid. [3]

---

1. http://en.wikipedia.org/wiki/Reliability_of_Wikipedia

2. Some of the phony journals claim to be peer-reviewed too. For example, the creationist organization Answers in Genesis publishes *Answers Research Journal*, supposedly peer-reviewed. Trouble is, the people doing the reviewing are as batshit as the people writing the articles.

3. A problem with the process is that other scientists tend to be busy doing their own research, and therefore only interested in attempting to replicate someone else's experiments if the results are fundamentally important. Results of minor concern far too often go unchecked. It would make a significant contribution to scientific progress, and thus to the GDP, if governments could establish institutions dedicated to attempting replications of published results. But then of course all the usual suspects would scream about the "waste" of taxpayers' money.

Occasionally, errors slip past the peer reviewers, other experimenters find they can't replicate the results, or a reader notices that a paper (or part of a paper) has been plagiarized from elsewhere or that there is actual fraud involved. For these and other reasons, a journal may *retract* a paper that it has published: It warns all readers that the paper is suspect, removes it from online publication, and takes whatever other measures it can to make sure the false information isn't further disseminated. Retraction can happen fairly quickly; sometimes it takes years before a journal retracts a dubious piece of work. It took until 2004, for example, for the medical journal *Lancet* to retract the 1998 paper it had published by Andrew Wakefield and others claiming that the MMR vaccine caused autism (see page 164).

A major problem with the modern scientific process is that negative results tend not to get published. If you've discovered a way to extract usable energy from drinking water, you obviously want to tell the world your results, and the scientific journals will likely be tripping over themselves with offers to publish them. If, by contrast, you do extensive research trying to extract cheap energy from water but fail in that quest, chances are you won't bother writing up your results; even if you do, it's likely no one will want to publish them. After all, who's interested in experiments that merely confirm what everyone assumed was the case? Yet those results can often be useful in themselves. If your paper recounted all the unsuccessful methods you'd tried, it could save later researchers a lot of time and effort.

Another problem with the scientific process was summed up by Albert Einstein:

> Because the academic career puts a young person in a
> sort of compulsory situation to produce scientific papers
> in impressive quantity, a temptation to superficiality aris-
> es that only strong characters are able to resist.

Modern academics are under strong pressure to produce lots of published papers to bring renown to the institution where they work (so the
reasoning goes). Often their jobs can depend on how many papers they
publish, whether or not those papers are useful. It's a case of "publish
or perish."

The result is that, as many scientists complain, far too many papers
are published that don't have anything new or important to say. This
obviously damages the scientific enterprise as a whole, because it's quite
possible for genuinely significant work to go unnoticed in the blizzard
of trivia. Aside from anything else, it means too often scientists are writing superfluous papers and working to get them published when they
could be better employed doing actual science.

EVALUATING SOURCES

In the previous chapter, we talked about the form of the argument from
authority in which the bullshitter cites dozens of irrelevant books and
papers as "authorities." The reason the trick often fools people is that it
looks very much like the perfectly respectable practice of citing *relevant*
sources in support of a viewpoint.

If you go to the hospital for a blood test using a note from your
bank manager as an authorization, the nurses will laugh at you. If

you go with a prescription from your doctor as authorization, out come the syringes. Both bank manager and doctor are authorities, but only the doctor is relevant in this instance. Likewise, if a TV talking head tells you not to worry about climate change while the assembled climate scientists of the IPCC[1] tell you it's a major emergency, it's easy enough to work out which is the more relevant authority. Often, though, evaluating your authorities—sources—can be a bit more difficult.

If you're checking something in the sciences, the best place to *start* is often Wikipedia. If you're trying to evaluate something that was published in a science journal, Wikipedia offers—as we saw (page 72)—a quick way of checking if the journal is respectable or bogus.

Otherwise, though, you should always be a bit suspicious of using a Wikipedia article as a reliable source of information. They're often surprisingly good, and for straight data they're as accurate as any you'll find—if you want to know the number of home runs Babe Ruth hit, look no further than his Wikipedia entry—but often they contain errors, and sometimes glaring ones. (The Wikipedia editors can't be correcting everywhere at once!) Here's the key: The real value of Wikipedia as a tool in evaluating sources lies less in the articles, and more in the sources that the articles offer.

Once you've established that the source you're checking actually exists (and sometimes bullshitters just invent them, knowing that hardly anyone will trouble to check) and that the journal the paper appeared in is reputable, the next thing to do is find the paper itself. Almost all reputable scholarly journals now post an *abstract* of every paper they

---

1. Intergovernmental Panel on Climate Change—see page 195.

publish online for free.[1] The abstract is a summary; essentially, the researchers state the question they set out to answer, the experiment(s) they did, and the conclusions they came to. Abstracts are often dry and jargon-ridden, but with a bit of effort most of them can be deciphered.

The point of reading the abstract is to check that the paper actually says what the suspected bullshitter claims it does. You'd be surprised how often it doesn't.

Of course, many times the sources you want to evaluate aren't obscure scholarly papers. Often information comes from newspapers, online news outlets, and TV news. Take a look at the outlet's history, biases, and what other kinds of reporting it does; this will help you figure out if you value it as a trusted source.

Always remember that you yourself are a source that needs to be evaluated. Whenever you judge information, you do so through a filter that's made up of your own preconceived ideas—a whole lifetime's worth of them. You can't hope to escape from those biases entirely, but you can at least learn to recognize them. If you continue to hear things that bolster one or more of your biases, it's worth standing back for a moment to make sure you aren't being fed a line of bullshit.

And remember, too, that a whole stack of unreliable sources never adds up to a single reliable one.[2] You can find a million people in cafes who'll tell you that AIDS only affects gay men but, if *Scientific American* says otherwise (which it does), it doesn't take a whole lot of critical thinking to work out who to believe.

---

1. Sometimes you can find the whole paper, but don't count on it. And sometimes authors/journals will put online a copy of the paper in "pre-publication."

2. Well, to *two* reliable ones. It's always a good idea to cross-check even the best-accredited authorities!

CONFIRMATION BIAS AND
MOTIVATED REASONING

These are two closely related traps into which it's far too easy to fall—and all of us do sometimes fall into one or the other.

The term *confirmation bias* refers to the tendency we have to notice things that reinforce our beliefs and fail to notice things that would undermine them. Even more alarmingly, if you set out looking for evidence that your beliefs are true, you may sooner or later start finding it everywhere you look!

To take an example that's close to home, there have almost certainly been times when you've disliked someone enough that, the way you saw it, there was literally nothing they could do right. They smiled and said hello to you in the street? They were laughing at you. They offered to help you with your homework? They were being condescending. A few months later you probably looked back on your former self and realized how biased you'd been. But, at the time, all the evidence seemed to indicate that the person deserved your dislike.

Where this kind of interpersonal confirmation bias becomes harmful on a massive scale is in its contribution to racial and other ethnic tension. People of one ethnic group (let's call them the Rounds) get it into their heads that people of another (the Squares) are always violent, or bullying, or dishonest, or sly—pick whatever unsavory human characteristic you want. From that point on, every time a Round sees a couple of Squares fighting, that's confirmation of the violent nature of all Squares.

But hang on a minute! What about all the *other* Squares, the ones who *aren't* fighting?

The confirmation bias kicks in again. The Squares who aren't fighting *aren't doing enough to stop the ones who are*! That just goes to show that they're really supporting the fighters, which is yet another piece of evidence that Squares are fundamentally violent by nature . . .

Motivated reasoning is very similar—and equally hard to recognize when you're doing it. Imagine you're confronted by a problem of some kind—say, what *is* the moon made of? Rather than looking at all the evidence, you decide the answer first—it's made of blue cheese—and go out in search of evidence to support your case, ignoring anything that might suggest you're wrong.

A good example is the frenzy that erupts periodically over the issue of voter fraud. We're told that voter fraud—people voting twice, for example—is a serious problem. And it's easy enough to find evidence, if you choose to look only at sources that will support the contention. Sometimes, for instance, there are people who are registered to vote in more than one state. What better indication could there be of a dishonest voting intent? The trouble with this argument is that, as any polling official will tell you, when people move from state A to state B, it can often take two or three electoral cycles before their information is scrubbed from the register in state A. There's no intent to defraud; it's just that the bureaucracy can be slow to catch up with the reality. Similarly, people can remain on the register for years after they've died.

In fact, voter fraud is not so much a serious problem as it is a virtually nonexistent one. In 2012, when Pennsylvania was pursuing a voter ID policy that could have disenfranchised tens of thousands of voters on the pretext that voter fraud was rampant, the state was forced to admit in court that it could find *no examples at all* of the crime having been committed!

How do you avoid confirmation bias and motivated reasoning? It's not hard—just difficult to remember to avoid it. Whenever you come to a conclusion, pause for a moment to ask yourself if you simply jumped to that conclusion or if you actually surveyed *all* the relevant evidence to get there, checking that evidence as you went along.

Remember, it's easier to get the crossword right if you've read the clues.

PATTERNS

One of the things our brains are very good at is recognizing patterns—in fact, it's a fundamental characteristic of human intelligence. Our distant ancestors recognized that the seasons followed a pattern through the year, and that so did the rising and setting of the stars in the night sky. Putting the two patterns together, our ancestors were able to tell when was the best time to plant their crops, or to hunt for mammoths. Millions of years later, that same ability to recognize patterns is what makes some people better at chess than others. Music, math, art, sports—there are patterns in almost all human activities, and our competence in detecting them quickly can be a tremendous advantage in problem-solving. Sometimes we do it unconsciously, in which case we call it intuition, or hunch (or, very misleadingly, instinct).

Unfortunately, it's far too easy to see patterns that aren't in fact there. How often do those hunches of ours actually pay off? If you're like me, surprisingly infrequently. It took me years to learn how lousy my hunch success rate was, because of course I tended only to remember the ones that were successful—the more successful they were, the more I was likely to remember them.

Whenever you feel a hunch coming on, pause and ask yourself if you have any rational cause to act on it.[1]

Bullshitters often rely on the fact that we tend to trust our intuition far more than we should. They present themselves in a guise that they think most people will intuitively trust —the kind-eyed, genial evangelist, the bluff, seemingly authoritative TV commentator, the politician who's all heart (yeah, right)—and let our assumptions do the rest. We see aspects of the bullshitter that fit a pattern we've created in our minds, whether it's truth or baloney—"he's got presidential hair"— and, if we're not careful, we act accordingly.

LABELING AND STEREOTYPING

Because of pattern recognition, we tend to classify things—we put them in mental boxes to make it easier for us to think about them. For the most part this is an invaluable tool. Dogs come in all shapes and sizes, from chihuahuas to great danes, but the category "dog" isn't a random or un-useful one. If someone tells you they've got a new dog, you immediately know what they mean, even if the details need to be filled in.

We categorize stuff all the time. Since the earliest days we've sorted the plant and animal kingdoms into mental categories based on their characteristics—carnivores, herbivores, poisonous, smelly, et cetera— and it was a great leap forward for the biological sciences

---

1. Of course, this can be difficult to do in some contexts. If you have a hunch your tennis opponent is going to send the next ball down the line or cross-court, probably better to go with it.

when, in the eighteenth century, the Swedish botanist Karl von Linné (Carolus Linnaeus) introduced some rigor to taxonomy, as this scheme of classification is called. Without the recognition that there are different species, and that the relationships between them can be deduced, Darwin would have had considerable difficulty working out his theory of evolution by natural selection, if indeed it would have been possible at all.

Not all of our classifications are wise, though. The trouble arises when we rely on categorization as a substitute for thinking. Demagogues exploit the trick of persuading us to make false classifications of our fellow human beings. Most famously, the Nazis persuaded the German people that various subsets of the population (like Jews and Serbs, for instance) were not to be classified as fully human, and could thus be exterminated without qualm. This technique of *dehumanization* has been used to inspire genocidal attempts throughout history and all over the world: It was also responsible for the near-annihilation of the Native Americans and the Australian Aborigines, for example.

Here's a more everyday example: It's all too easy for liberals to dismiss someone as a "fascist" when really they're just a conservative. And, on the right, some critics of President Obama have been known to criticize him as socialist, Marxist, fascist, atheist, and Islamist *all at the same time*, even though these labels are mutually incompatible and not one of them is in fact demonstrably true.[1]

Soon after he was first elected, President George W. Bush cracked that "If this were a dictatorship, it would be a heck of a lot easier . . . just so long as I'm the dictator." It was a joke. Most of us have made

---

1. If in doubt, go look up "Marxism" in any decent dictionary.

similar jokes: "If I ruled the world . . ." Yet many liberal commentators pretended to take it at face value, and there were plenty among their audience who assumed Bush really *did* want to be a dictator. It was easier to stick the label "wannabe dictator" on him than to dissect his actual politics.

Labels and stereotypes take critical thinking out of the equation, which isn't good for anyone. Just like when you feel a hunch, or whenever you make a quick assumption about someone, you should ask yourself if it's based in rational fact, or based on a stereotype.

YOUR VERY OWN BULLSHITOMETER: A QUICK CHECKLIST

You read something in a book, you hear something on the radio, a TV commentator makes a statement, your irritating little brother tells you what *he* thinks . . . and your antenna starts to quiver because all of a sudden you detect

BULLSHIT!

Here's a handy checklist of the steps you can take when you think there's bullshit in the air . . .

- Ignore the flim-flam and focus on the substance. Page 9.
- Think about whether the authorities that someone's quoting really *are* authorities. Page 56.

- Check the context of the quotes that people present you. Are they in context? They could mean something quite different from what you thought when taken in the context of an entire speech or article. Page 48.
- Similarly, watch out for the straw man tactic. Page 52.
- Don't take data at face value if you're suspicious of the person presenting it to you. See if you can find the source of the *raw* data. Page 72.
- It's what people say or think that's important, not what they look like or what country they come from. Avoid labeling or stereotyping people. Page 80.
- The plural of "anecdote" isn't "evidence"! Page 58.
- If someone keeps shifting his ground (or "moving the goalposts") when he's trying to persuade you, be suspicious. Page 60.
- Be alert for false balance in news coverage. The balance point between rational and batshit crazy is . . . batshit crazy. Page 62.
- Just because you can't immediately explain something doesn't mean you have to believe the first "explanation" someone offers you. Take your time and do some more research. Page 63.
- Hunches are not your friends. If you find yourself jumping to conclusions, they're probably the wrong ones. Page 67.
- That impressive list of authorities someone produces in supposed support of what they're saying? Try to find time to fact-check at least a few of them. Page 56.

- If all the evidence you find seems to confirm your beliefs, pause for a moment to make sure you're being objective. Page 77.
- The word "theory" has several uses. If someone tries to tell you that a piece of established science—like evolution—is "just a theory," either they're ignorant or they're trying to bullshit you. Page 68.
- Wherever it makes sense to do so, apply the Scientific Method or some variant of it. It's probably the single most powerful component of your Bullshitometer. Page 66.

🚫

PART TWO

STALKING THE WILD BALONEY

1. NOBLE MONKEYS: WHERE WE CAME FROM

In early February 2014, a debate was held between the popular scientific broadcaster Bill Nye—"The Science Guy"—and Ken Ham, founder and president of the Creationist organization Answers in Genesis (AiG). Among its other activities, AiG runs the Creation Museum in Kentucky—whose displays include humans consorting with dinosaurs—and is currently (late 2014) trying to raise money to build a full-size replica of Noah's Ark. Inevitably, the debate was nicknamed "Ham on Nye"!

The topic of debate was: "Is creation a viable model of origins in today's modern, scientific era?" Of course, in all the press buzz surrounding the debate, the actual topic tended to get forgotten, so the debate was essentially billed as one between evolution and Creationism.

At the debate, Matt Stopera of the website *BuzzFeed* "asked 22 self-identifying Creationists . . . to write a message/question/note to the other side." The results ranged from the wacky to the bewildering. Here is a selection of the ones that caught my eye.:

> 1. Is it completely illogical that the earth was created mature? i.e. trees created with rings . . . Adam created as an adult . . .[1]

---

1. The ellipses, capitalizations, spellings, et cetera., are the writers', not mine. I've numbered the comments for ease of reference.

2. Does not the Second law of thermodynamics disprove evolution?

3. If God did not create everything, how did the first single-celled organism originate? By chance?

4. Why do evolutionists / secularists / humanists / non-God believing people reject the idea of their being a creator God but embrace the concept of intelligent design from aliens or other extra-terrestrial sources?

5. Why have we found only 1 "Lucy", when we have found more than one of everything else?

6. If Evolution is a theory (like creationism or the Bible) why then is Evolution taught as fact.

7. How can you look at the world and not believe Someone Created/thought of it? It's *Amazing!!!*

8. Relating to the big bang theory . . . Where did the exploding star come from?

9. How do you explain a sunset if their is no God?

10. What about Noetics?

11. Does metamorphosis support evolution?

and, inevitably,

12. If we came from monkeys then why are there still monkeys?

What's interesting about these comments is that, the wacky ones aside, they give a good overview of most of the main bits of bullshit that are leveled by today's Creationists—again and again, no matter how often the misapprehensions are corrected—against evolution.

Let's look at a few of these questions in a bit more detail.. First, though, a quick note on question #8: "Relating to the big bang theory . . . Where did the exploding star come from?"—*What* exploding star? If he meant to say "Where did the Big Bang come from?"—implying that everything must have a cause and so there must have been some entity that created the Big Bang—the next question we have to ask is: Where did *that entity* come from?

Just as importantly, what has the Big Bang got to do with the theory of evolution, which is concerned with living organisms on planet earth?[1]

IF EVOLUTION IS A THEORY (LIKE CREATIONISM OR THE BIBLE) WHY THEN IS EVOLUTION TAUGHT AS FACT?

This is a typical semantics game used by dishonest people to fool ignorant ones, and consequently by ignorant people to fool themselves.

As we've seen before, the word "theory" has three quite distinct meanings.[2] In general conversation, when we say we have a theory, we

---

1. Many creationists believe that the theory of evolution by natural selection purports to explain the origin of life and even the origin of the universe. It doesn't: Its sole concern is with the way that living things evolve. Even so, biologists are often challenged by creationists to explain the Big Bang; after all, say the creationists, it's impossible to get something (the universe) out of nothing. In fact, it's a question that physics can answer—and the theoretical physicist Lawrence M. Krauss wrote a book dedicated to that answer: *A Universe from Nothing: Why There is Something Rather than Nothing* (2012). The book's a bit technical in places, but it's quite short and well worth the effort.

2. There are a few more, but only three are relevant here.

mean little if anything more than an idea or hunch or point of view: "It's my theory that children should be seen and not heard."

Sometimes we use the word a bit more seriously to mean what we think is a plausible explanation for something. In scientific terms, this type of "theory" is more correctly called a hypothesis. The person who produced the question above is implying that the theory of evolution is only *this* kind of "theory": something speculative for which there's as yet only a scattering of evidence.

But that isn't at all what the word "theory" means when we talk about the theory of evolution by natural selection—or the theory of Special Relativity, or the quantum theory, and so on. In the full scientific sense of the word, as we saw when talking about the Scientific Method (see page 66), an established scientific theory is as close to a cast-iron fact as you're ever likely to find.

Beyond the definition of the word "theory," there's another sense in which the question is misguided. Evolution *itself* isn't a theory; it's an established fact. Not only can we see evolution in action, the interrelatedness of all living things has been demonstrated conclusively at the genetic level. The "theory" part is that evolution *works because of natural selection*. This was a theory first put forward in the nineteenth century by Charles Darwin and Alfred Russel Wallace in order to explain evolution. It has since been modified because of further scientific discovery, but is still fundamentally intact.

What did Darwin and Wallace mean by "natural selection"?

As life forms produce new generations, there will inevitably be small variations between one individual and another. In some cases, the difference will be big enough to be called a mutation—those two-headed calves you occasionally hear about represent quite extreme mutations.

The basic idea of natural selection is that disadvantageous mutations tend to die out (the individuals involved may not live long enough to breed, for example) while advantageous ones are more likely to be preserved.

The modifications to Darwin's theory are generally to the effect that natural selection is not the only process involved—that others make a contribution. Also, since Darwin couldn't know anything about genetics, he had no idea *how* mutations could arise, and thus that, for example, the genes for disadvantageous traits can hang around within a species rather than die out, so long as the disadvantage isn't too great. If circumstances change for the species, those traits can suddenly become useful.

An illustration of this occurred in the UK from the 1950s onward, when the authorities clamped down on the use of coal fires in homes. Before that, a species called the peppered moth had shown primarily dark-colored wings: Windowsills and other likely resting places were dark from soot, and so the moths were less likely to be noticed and eaten by passing birds. A few moth-generations after the clampdown, however, the prevalent form of the peppered moth now had pale wings, because resting surfaces were cleaner and birds were less likely to notice light-colored moths.

So evolution isn't a theory, it's a fact of life. And evolution by natural selection isn't "just a theory": It's a *theory*.

HOW DID THE FIRST SINGLE-CELLED ORGANISM ORIGINATE? BY CHANCE?

This question actually has nothing to do with evolution. Evolution didn't start until after that very first living organism came into being.[1] The science of evolution is about what happens to life forms, not about how life arose.

The confusion is probably because of the title of the book in which Charles Darwin laid out the hypothesis at which he and Alfred Russel Wallace had independently arrived: *On the Origin of Species by Means of Natural Selection, or the Preservation of Favoured Races in the Struggle for Life* (1859), usually called just *Origin of Species*. A lot of people think this means the book is about the origin of life. In fact it's about why *species* originate—why there are millions of species of living creatures in the world, some more closely related than others.

So how *did* the first living organism emerge? It's a good question, because all of us—people and bananas and bacteria and kangaroos and birds and mosquitoes alike—are descended from that primordial organism. The answer is that science doesn't yet know for sure.

When this question was asked at the Ham/Nye debate, the questioner probably thought that, since science doesn't know, the only possible answer must be that the primordial organism was created rather than developed through natural processes. This is the notorious god of the gaps argument again (see page 63).

---

1. You could say that the chemical processes that led up to the emergence of that first organism represent evolution in a different sense of the word, but that's another story.

The questioner's also spinning the truth. Just because science doesn't know how life *did* start, doesn't mean science can't think of any way how it *could* have started. The reality is that there are plenty of plausible hypotheses as to how it happened; it's just that no one yet knows which if any of them is the *right* one!

No good scientist will tell you it's impossible that the first organism was created. What any good scientist will tell you is that there's zilch evidence in favor of that hypothesis.

DOESN'T THE SECOND LAW OF THERMODYNAMICS DISPROVE EVOLUTION?

The Second Law of Thermodynamics is popularly believed to say that everything tends—like your bedroom—to become more disorganized over time. So the argument goes that, since evolution is evidently a process of organization, it runs counter to the Second Law—in other words, it is impossible.

What the Second Law *actually* says is that, in an isolated (or closed) system, entropy (which means roughly the same as "disorganization") will always increase. A closed system is one where there's no energy coming in or going out.

The universe is a closed system, yet wherever we look there are examples of things that are more organized than they once were. Stars are more organized than the gas clouds from which they condensed. Inside stars, simple atomic nuclei are fused together to form more complicated—more organized—ones. When solar systems form, some planets are mainly rocky while others are mainly gaseous—in other words, there is a sorting process in play.

But these decreases in entropy are only part of the story. Those "organized" stars are at the same time converting matter into raw energy. If they're large enough, toward the end of their lifetimes they'll explode, throwing much of themselves out into space to join the disorganized interstellar gas while the rest collapses into a highly entropic black hole or a neutron star. All sorts of other processes act to increase entropy.

Overall, then, the universe's entropy is increasing: There's more disorganization going on than there is organization.

As a rule of thumb, the way to make anything less disorganized is to do work on it. It takes a lot more energy to sort out a bag of marbles into their different colors than it does simply to leave them in their disorganized state. A planet like the earth is more organized than all the floating rocks and dust and gas that came together to form it because of the work done by gravitational energy.

And the earth isn't a closed system: there's energy coming in from outside, and there's energy going out again. Among other exchanges with the rest of the universe, the earth receives great amounts of sunlight. When this energy is eventually radiated back into space, it's in the form of high-entropy heat. The sunlight is the fuel that powers organizational processes on earth, processes like life and evolution. Because our planet isn't a closed system, the Second Law of Thermodynamics doesn't apply.

IF WE EVOLVED FROM MONKEYS, WHY ARE THERE STILL MONKEYS?

Ask any evolutionary biologist and they'll tell you this is the single most common question they get asked by creationists. No matter how often they answer it, it gets repeated again and again, like a dripping tap. It's a question that reveals a lack of knowledge not just about how evolution works, but also about our own primate ancestry. Oddly, the people who ask it—the primate-change deniers—never think to ask themselves the question's corollary: If we *didn't* evolve from other primates, why are there other primates?

The first thing to be clear on is that no serious scientist says we evolved from modern monkeys. Monkeys and humans have about 93 percent of their DNA coding in common, which means we're not all that distantly related to monkeys. On the other hand, we're not all that *closely* related to them either. The primate species that both ourselves and monkeys evolved from—our common ancestor—lived about 25–30 million years ago. The earliest known monkeys (that is, mammals that were related to the monkeys we know today) date to about 15 million years ago.

Monkeys, like every other life form on the planet, are still evolving, of course. But what they're evolving into is not humans, but *different monkeys*.

We're far more closely related to chimps and gorillas, who are not monkeys but apes. We share more than 98 percent of our DNA coding with chimps. The common ancestor of chimps and humans lived perhaps 4.7 million years ago. That was long after the ape and monkey lineages had gone their separate ways.

Apes are still evolving, too . . . into *different apes*.

But there's another huge misunderstanding in the question. The type of ape that chimps and ourselves evolved from is long extinct, as are the other types of apes that existed 4.7 million years ago. Newer types of apes have appeared as the older types died out. The array of ape species 4.7 million years ago was different from what's around today.

Similarly, in a million years, if humans are still around, they will be very different from the way we are today. The idea that humans are still evolving is one that many people have difficulty grasping. The way we are today is just the way a particular strand of our planet's evolving biosphere has ended up by the twenty-first century. All of the animals that frequent my back yard—bears, chipmunks, turkeys, hawks, foxes, squirrels, cardinals, gophers, lizards, and countless others—are as highly evolved as I am, and as you are. A fox is far better at being a fox than you or I would be.

INTELLIGENT DESIGN FROM OUTER SPACE?

There's one last question to be answered from the list asked by Ken Ham's supporters. It's a longer one, so I'll state it again:

> Why do evolutionists / secularists / humanists / non-God believing people reject the idea of their [*sic*] being a creator God but embrace the concept of intelligent design from aliens or other extra-terrestrial sources?

The questioner seems to have gotten two things confused.

A few decades back, various amateur archaeologists—and that's the polite description—started promoting the idea that alien astronauts visited the earth thousands of years ago, boosted the primitive human civilizations then in existence, and even tinkered with the brains of our ancestors to make them smarter. These theorists made a truckload of money writing books and making TV shows; they're still making the TV shows, although the books aren't as common. What they didn't do was persuade many (if any!) reputable scientists, and particularly not professional archaeologists and anthropologists, who could find no trace of the supposed extraterrestrial interference.[1]

The questioner has mixed this crankery up with the far more recent Intelligent Design (ID) movement.

During the nineteenth century, evolution was an idea that was very much discussed, and a number of naturalists, like the Chevalier de Lamarck (see page 110), put forward their own ideas about how it could work. Theologians, however, stuck to the notion of intelligent design, which posited that, since living creatures had multiple components and were generally suited to their mode of existence, it was "obvious" they must have been designed to be that way. As long ago as the thirteenth century, Thomas Aquinas presented this "obvious" influence of a Designer as one of his five irrefutable proofs of the existence of God.

What governed mainstream scientific opinion for most of the nineteenth century was the case in favor of intelligent design put forward by William Paley in his book *Natural Theology, or Evidences of the Existence and Attributes of the Deity Collected from the Appearances of*

---

1. For more on the ancient astronauts hypothesis, see page 247.

Nature (1802). In vivid fashion he argued that, if you find a functioning watch, you rationally assume there must be a watchmaker somewhere. Similarly, Paley said, if you come across a functioning life form or a functioning organ—like the human eye—you should rationally assume the existence of a designer.

Before Charles Darwin and Alfred Russel Wallace came along with their theory of evolution by natural selection, which quite comfortably explained (among much else) how organs like the human eye developed without supernatural intervention, there wasn't much of a controversy between religious explanations of life and the ideas of naturalists. In his book *God's Own Scientists* (1994), Christopher P. Toumey summed this up: "Evangelical Protestantism and science were so intellectually compatible in the United States that a naturalist and a minister could easily agree on what they believed about nature." Even today, plenty of naturalists and plenty of ministers find they can *still* agree about nature,[1] but some still have more difficulty.

The modern ID movement was the brainchild not of a scientist but of a lawyer (evaluate your authorities!), Phillip Johnson, who made his case in a book called *Darwin on Trial* (1991). Johnson believed religion was steadily losing its status in the United States, and he blamed this on science education in public schools. The villain, in his mind, was the theory of evolution by natural selection. A whole series of court decisions had made it impossible for Creationism to be taught in science classrooms (it violates the First Amendment), and so Johnson realized he'd have to offer a "scientific" theory that, with luck, could get round the prohibition. Intelligent Design was the result.

---

1. "If God chooses evolution as His method, who are we to argue?"

ID accepts that the bulk of the changes that come about in life forms—such as separation into different species—are a result of evolution. However, it proposes that, at crucial moments, an unspecified supernatural being steps in to tweak the process a little. These extra little tweaks explain, the IDers claim, various developments that unguided evolution could not have achieved alone.

An important extra concept here is "irreducible complexity," first proposed by the biochemist Michael Behe. Take a feature like the mammalian eye. It's made up of a number of parts—lens, retina, and so on—that must work together if the eye is to function properly. Each of those parts wouldn't be much use on its own. How could the lens, for example, survive as a mutation if it didn't have the other components of the eye to go with it? And how could the fully formed eye simply spring into being from nowhere?

So Behe's idea was that features like the eye are *irreducibly complex*. Because they can't work unless all the bits are there, an Intelligent Designer must have intervened to bring them together in just the right way.

Often IDers seek to demonstrate this point by showing you the components of a mousetrap and asking you how effective you think they'd be at catching a mouse. As soon as you point out that they couldn't—you'd have to assemble them first—you get told this is because the mousetrap is irreducibly complex. You need a Designer to assemble it . . . and, in the same way, you need a Designer to assemble something like the eye. Until the mousetrap/eye is assembled, what would be the point of its components having evolved separately?

What's forgotten in discussions of irreducible complexity is that natural selection is very good at making opportunistic use of whatever happens to be lying around. In the case of the evolution of the eye,

Darwin pointed out in *Origin of Species* how the various stages could have come about, starting off with just a light-sensitive cell. All of the progressively more complex stages that Darwin outlined have been observed in living creatures, so we know they're possible. In fact, we now know that at various times in various creatures, over forty different types of eye have evolved, each independently of the others.

In a famous trial in Dover, Pennsylvania, in 2005 about the teaching of ID in the classroom, Michael Behe was called as a witness in favor of the case that ID had a scientific basis and therefore could legitimately be taught alongside evolution. He naturally presented his idea of irreducible complexity as a clincher. Unfortunately, under cross-examination he was forced to admit that all of the features he claimed as irreducibly complex have in fact been explained perfectly adequately by biologists without the need to resort to the intervention of the Designer. You could say this isn't *proof* that a Designer didn't play a part. True. But it's also not proof that the Easter Bunny wasn't involved, or the Man in the Moon. The general rule in science is, if there's no evidence that something exists, then it almost certainly doesn't. If somebody thinks it exists nevertheless, the burden's on them to show it does, not on everyone else to show it doesn't.

The vanguard of the ID movement is the Discovery Institute, founded in 1996 and based in Seattle. In 1999 this "think tank" set up an offshoot called the Center for the Renewal of Science & Culture; in 2002 this was renamed the Center for Science & Culture. It's this offshoot, with its sciencey-sounding name, that does the main work of promoting ID.

One of its big embarrassments is that, for a supposed scientific institute, it doesn't seem to do much if any scientific research. If you go to its website[1] you can find a list of published scientific papers purportedly supporting ID. If you dig a little deeper, however, you discover that the "peer-reviewed" journals many of these papers appeared in are, shall we say, at a bit of a distance from the mainstream. Also, if you look closely at the papers, you'll see there's little or no *research* involved in them. You can find the generation of concepts like irreducible complexity, but these are really philosophical notions, not scientific hypotheses backed by experimental evidence. And there are plenty of attempts to find fault with mainstream evolutionary theory—attempts that are essentially worthless because biologists have confronted all of them many long ages ago.

The Discovery Institute is keen on calling ID a *theory* (see page 67). Without much if any research being done to test it or to gather data that might support or otherwise affect it, it's hard to see how the word "theory" can be applied.

All in all, the Discovery Institute's really in the same position, so far as scientific research goes, as that boring guy at the party (or, for that matter, on talk radio) who boasts that he knows more about biology than biologists do, more about medicine than doctors do, more about climate science than climate scientists do . . . all without having had to go to the trouble of doing any study!

A second big embarrassment for the Discovery Institute's claims to be advancing the course of science is the existence of the Wedge Document. This was a strategy cooked up in the Center for the Renewal of Science & Culture sometime in the late 1990s. Soon after, it leaked to the web. What's clear on reading the document is that the ID move-

---

1. http://www.discovery.org/csc/.

ment's questioning of the rationale of Darwinism is intended solely as an opening salvo—the thin end of a wedge whose thick end is the replacement of science ("materialism") by theology.

In 2001 the Discovery Institute released a document grandly called *A Scientific Dissent from Darwinism*, signed by several hundred scientists. The July 2013 update of that statement contained (if I counted right) the names of 841 scientists from all over the world who query the theory of evolution by natural selection. If you look down the list you find that, while many of the signatories work in the field of biology, many don't—there are plenty of engineers and surgeons there. Wow: 841! That seems a very large number until you realize that *in the US alone* there are perhaps 3,500,000 working scientists and engineers—and that doesn't include physicians. When you put 841 alongside 3,500,000 you realize what a small number it actually is.

Back to the original question: When the questioner stated that evolutionary scientists "embrace the concept of intelligent design from aliens or other extra-terrestrial sources," we can only guess that no one has ever told him that natural selection works without the need for external tinkering. Having learned that scientists reject the idea that a supernatural being tweaks the system from time to time, he's jumped to the conclusion that they must instead believe in crackpot ideas about ancient astronauts.

WHAT'S THE DIFFERENCE BETWEEN MICRO-EVOLUTION AND MACRO-EVOLUTION?

Creationists often say they can accept the idea of *micro*-evolution but not that of *macro*-evolution. What do these terms mean?

Micro-evolution is change within a species. You can get an idea of what micro-evolution is about by looking at dogs. You get dogs of every shape and size, but they're all still dogs—they all belong to the same species. No matter how different they might appear, any type of dog can breed with any other, as you can tell by a quick visit to the local pound. (There might be practical difficulties with dogs of vastly different sizes, but theoretically it's possible.) You can think of the different breeds having arisen through micro-evolution; even though the different breeds of dogs have arisen almost entirely due to artificial selection (deliberate breeding) rather than natural selection, the principle's the same. Micro-evolution is change within a species.

Macro-evolution involves the emergence of new species. You can mate a terrier with a spaniel, for example, to produce viable puppies, and you can even mate a dog with a wolf (they're both members of the species *Canis lupus*), but you can't mate a dog with a cat. Dogs and cats share a common ancestor, but that common ancestor lived upward of 40 million years ago. Today dogs and cats aren't just in different species, they're in different genera and families.[1]

---

1. Going downward, the various taxonomies used to categorize living organisms are domain, kingdom (animal, plant, et cetera.), phylum, class, order, family, genus, species, subspecies. Both dogs and cats are of the order Carnivora, but dogs are in the family Canidae and cats in the family Felidae.

It's obviously difficult to deny micro-evolution, because we can see it going on, but most Creationists balk at the idea that new species can emerge from old ones.

Of course, this causes the Creationists problems if, as many do, they believe in the Flood, and that Noah took two of every type of non-aquatic animal aboard the Ark. With so many millions of species in the world today, how could this have been possible? It becomes even *more* difficult once you start counting in the extinct species, like mammoths and velociraptors. Some of those animals were *huge*.

A tactic that's used by many Creationists, such as Ken Ham, is to claim that Noah took aboard only two of each "kind" of the animals and that, after the Flood, the offspring of these pairs gave rise to the multitudinous species we see today. So the idea is that evolution within a "kind" is feasible (micro-evolution), but not the generation of a new "kind" (macro-evolution). Unfortunately, no one else can work out what this spanky new animal classification—the "kind"—actually *is*.

From the viewpoint of orthodox biology, rather than Creationist biology, it's obvious enough that, in simplest terms, macro-evolution is merely micro-evolution writ large. If you're prepared to accept that the micro happens, you have no rational grounds for rejecting the macro.

WHAT ABOUT THE CAMBRIAN EXPLOSION?

The fossil record shows that about 540 million years ago there was a sudden proliferation of complex lifeforms. This was the so-called Cambrian explosion, and a lot of creationists and especially IDers point to it as something that can't be explained through the slow processes of natural selection. Surely, they argue, there must have been some outside agency at work. Books like Stephen C. Meyer's *Darwin's Doubt: The Explosive Origin of Animal Life and the Case for Intelligent Design* (2013) back this up—as you'd expect, since Meyer was a co-founder of the Discovery Institute's Center for Science & Culture (see page 100).

Mainstream biologists are less impressed.

For a start, how sudden was this "sudden" explosion? It's difficult to estimate a timespan when people disagree about the start and stop points of the event but, at a very minimum, the "explosion" lasted about five million years and, according to some, as long as 40 million years. Even five million years marks an event not quite so "sudden" as you might have been led to believe.

And, although the Cambrian explosion was a period of relatively rapid evolution and a significant event in the history of life, it wasn't so pivotal as it's often portrayed:

- There's evidence of complex lifeforms from long beforehand, so the ones that now appeared were far from unprecedented.
- While some of the major animal groups can trace their origins to the Cambrian explosion, most don't: Mammals, reptiles, and insects were long in the future, and even more so birds, which are of reptilian descent. There were fishes, but their resemblances to modern fishes were scant. The first land plants didn't happen along until about 450 million years ago—that's nearly 100 million years after the "explosion"—and the first flowers probably not until about 130 million years ago.

IF EVOLUTION IS REAL, WHY ISN'T IT HAPPENING NOW?

It is. It's happening everywhere around us. Anyone who asks you this question really doesn't understand what evolution's all about. They might even follow up with some absurdity to the effect that, if evolution were real, we should expect cats to be giving birth to dogs.

Natural selection is usually a slow process, when measured in lifetimes; the more complicated the life form, the slower the process is likely to be. When voyagers from Europe arrived in the Americas, for example, they discovered people who'd been separated from the rest of humanity for many thousands of years, yet the differences were superficial.

But this doesn't mean that human evolution isn't still happening. The same goes for the evolution of other organisms. When you look at simpler creatures with far shorter lifetimes, like bacteria, you can see evolution happening very quickly. The reason that antibiotics eventually become less effective is that the bacteria they once could kill have evolved to resist them.

No one knows for sure why the Cambrian explosion happened, but this doesn't mean it's a glaring anomaly in terms of evolution. There are plenty of alternative explanations that don't require the intervention of an Intelligent Designer. A couple of possibilities are:

- The first evolution of eyes. Eyes would allow predators to become far more efficient, so prey animals had to become better at escaping or otherwise avoiding getting eaten. This could certainly have spurred adaptation.
- The first appearance of the ozone layer. This layer high in the earth's atmosphere protects the surface (and us!) from most of the lethal radiation that comes our way from space.

So, while there's still lots of research to be done on the Cambrian explosion, it's by no means as inexplicable as the IDers pretend.

DARWIN CAUSED THE HOLOCAUST?

Time and time again, Creationists accuse the theory of evolution by natural selection—and Darwin by name—of having inspired the Nazis to murder millions of Jews, gays, gypsies, and others, including the mentally ill.

The accusation would have surprised the Nazis, because official Party policy rejected evolution. During the Reich, science was under the control of Heinrich Himmler, and Himmler refused to believe that

- humans could have evolved from lower animals,
- humans were related to the primates, and even
- modern *Homo sapiens* could have arisen from Neanderthals.

DIDN'T WE ALL COME FROM ADAM AND EVE?

A population bottleneck happens to a species when, for any of a number of reasons, its population plunges to a fraction of its former level. If the numbers are still large enough to maintain a viable breeding population, the species may survive and become prolific again. If the numbers fall too low, however, the species goes extinct.

Unfortunately for a literal reading of *Genesis*, two individuals isn't a viable breeding population for human beings—or indeed for any other higher primate. Of course, we could still argue that humans are a special case, given divine assistance to establish themselves. Genetic studies have, however, given us a fairly clear record of population sizes ever since our ancestors split off from the ancestors of the chimps.

It turns out there have been two significant bottlenecks in that period. Between about four and three million years ago, there was a sudden drop from a very large population to a mere 10,000 or so. The population remained at about that level, growing gently to about 16,000, then began falling off again about 100,000 years ago. All this happened in Africa.

From perhaps about 40,000 years ago, some groups of humans began leaving Africa to colonize the rest of the world. Around 10,000–20,000 years ago, the human populations both inside and outside of Africa bottlenecked considerably, so there were just a few thousand humans left; of those humans living outside Africa, the number appears to have been not much over 1,200.

These are frighteningly small numbers—a single outbreak of some nasty disease could have wiped out the human species entirely! But a few thousand is still a whole lot more than two.

Since displeasing Himmler was a fast track to the concentration camps, most German scientists toed the Party line.

What the Nazis *did* believe in was eugenics. Eugenics is based on the idea that—just as farmers breed their animals for better qualities—you can create "better" humans by weeding out all the "undesirables" from the breeding pool. The big problem with eugenics, obviously, is: Who decides who the "undesirables" are? Eugenics was promoted by Charles Darwin's cousin, Francis Dalton, but Darwin himself firmly rejected it as unthinkably cruel and immoral.

The notion of eugenics was responsible for widespread atrocities during the first half of the twentieth century, not just in Germany but in other countries, notably the US and Sweden, though only Germany instituted mass exterminations. The more usual approach involved campaigns of forced sterilization. In the US, support for eugenics and forced-sterilization campaigns didn't really collapse until after the end of World War II, when the public learned of the German atrocities.

THE SURVIVAL OF THE FITTEST

Evolution *isn't* about the survival of the fittest.[1]

You may be shocked to hear this, because so many detractors of evolution and even some of its ardent supporters think this notion is at the core of how natural selection works. Evolution is really about populations, not about individual members of those populations. This

---

1. Obviously we don't mean "fittest" here in the sense of who's got the best abs. In this context the word "fittest" means something like "best adapted to the circumstances."

can be difficult to accept in human societies that are concerned about individual as well as group welfare, but it's the way nature works. As with eugenics, attempts to take the *descriptions* of evolution and make them into *prescriptions* for the way that human societies should be run inevitably lead to gross cruelty and misery on a grand scale.

Darwin himself didn't employ the phrase "survival of the fittest" and it's not one that's used in modern evolutionary biology (except perhaps in the case of genes). No one's sure exactly who coined it, but it was first popularized by the UK philosopher/economist Herbert Spencer. Excited by Darwin's theory but perhaps even more so by those of the Chevalier de Lamarck,[1] Spencer wrote a book called *Principles of Biology* (1864) in which he attempted to marry natural selection to his own notions of how society should be run. Those notions—that we should expect and accept that the privileged and ruthless will rise to the top of society, with the rest of us either in servitude to them or going to the wall—were much later called Social Darwinism. This term is grossly misleading, in that it implies that the scientific theory of evolution justifies human hardship and economic tyranny, but unfortunately it has stuck.

The confusion is exploited by creationists to this day. Although Spencer's ideas were, for some while during the early part of the twentieth century, all the rage among the "robber baron" industrialists of the US (oddly enough, they never much caught on in his native land), they became mightily unpopular after World War II when, as with eugenics, the consequences became all too horrifically obvious.

---

1. Lamarck suggested that features acquired by a creature during its lifetime could be passed on to its offspring. Before Darwin and Wallace recognized the principle of natural selection, Lamarck's hypothesis attracted a lot of interest. However, since tattooed parents don't give birth to tattooed babies, to choose just a single example, it was eventually discarded.

YOUNG EARTH OR OLD EARTH?

In modern Creationism, there are two schools of thought about the age of the earth.

Old-earth Creationists (OECs) accept that the universe and the earth are of great antiquity, and regard the "days" mentioned in *Genesis* as periods of uncertain but great length. (This is a viable translation of the original text.)

Young-earth creationists (YECs) insist the earth was created just a few thousand years ago. Today, the usual figure they offer for the planet's age is about 10,000 years. The young-earth creationist Harold Camping, famous for unsuccessfully predicting the end of the world in 2011 (see page 269), calculated the earth was about 13,000 years old, and the nineteenth-century German scholar Christian von Bunsen produced a figure of 22,000 years. Meanwhile a few YECs have suggested that that is far younger than any of these estimates.

What's puzzling is that all these calculations are supposedly based on the same data. It's perhaps not so surprising that such problems occur when trying to use the Bible as a science textbook. In *1 Kings* 7/23-6, for example, the value of pi, the ratio between a circle's circumference and its diameter, is indicated to be exactly 3.0.

Mainstream science offers a far different estimate of the world's age. The oldest known crystal, a tiny piece of zircon found in early 2014 on a Western Australia sheep ranch, has been confidently dated to 4.4 billion years ago.

$\oslash$

2. THE WONDERFUL POWER OF WOO

> Why do you think that 1 percent of the population earns
> around 96 percent of all the money that's being earned?
> Do you think that's an accident? It's designed that way.
> They understand something. They understand *The Secret*.

The above paragraph, written by Bob Proctor, comes from a book called *The Secret* (2006), edited by Australian TV producer Rhonda Byrne, which was a huge bestseller a few years ago. The "secret" that Byrne's numerous contributors are talking about is that, if you wish for something hard enough, your wish will immediately permeate every corner of the universe; and the universe, hearing your wish, will grant it.

And if you don't do the wishing just exactly the right way, the universe will do the *opposite* of what you want to happen. This is because the universe, which we must assume suffers learning difficulties, can't distinguish between these two possibilities:

- You're thinking about something because you want it to happen.
- You're thinking about something because you *don't* want it to happen.

This leaves you with some difficult choices to make. Should surfers make a wish that they don't get attacked by sharks? After all, the universe might interpret this wrongly and send in a flotilla of the beasts. Should Olympic athletes wish for a gold medal, knowing their wish might guarantee they finish in last place? Is it a good idea to hope your lunch won't give you food poisoning?

Presumably, Byrne and her contributors hoped *The Secret* would make them a lot of money, and it worked for *them*.

The book, which has a matching DVD, is full of valuable morsels for the dedicated bullshit hunter, such as that "Abraham, Isaac, Jacob, Joseph, Moses and Jesus were not only prosperity teachers but also millionaires" and that "Every thought has a frequency. We can measure a thought." There's even a bit of cosmology: "Quantum physicists tell us that the entire Universe emerged from thought."

It's fairly obvious *The Secret* is woo—and proudly so!—from start to finish. Its con trick is equally obvious: If the Secret doesn't work for you, that's not because it's nonsense but because *you didn't do it right*. This has some pretty revolting consequences, as many people pointed out at the time. Do you *really* think the Holocaust was the fault of millions of Jews for harboring negative thoughts?

IGNORING THE FAILURES

The idea at the core of *The Secret*—that if you wish for something hard enough it'll surely come true—is a classic example of what's called *magical thinking*. There's not really a whole lot of difference, in terms of irrationality, between *The Secret* and, for example, Donald L. Wilson's 1979 book *Total Mind Power: How to Use the Other 90% of Your Mind to Increase the Size of Your Breasts*. Both rely on the gullibility of readers who believe they can bring things about by the power of mind alone.

It's something we all do from time to time. Are you telepathic? Even if you don't think so now, the likelihood is that you did at some stage. Do you think praying for someone who's sick will help them get better? Do you offer up a few earnest wishes to your guardian angel the night before a test—even if you don't really believe in guardian angels? Do you put your trust in a lucky baseball cap? Do you cross your fingers before you toss a coin?

The central character of "The Nun's Priest's Tale" by the medieval poet Geoffrey Chaucer is a rooster called Chanticleer who believes the sun rises each day just to hear him crow. Of course, we know the sun would rise whether or not there were roosters there to crow at it, but Chaucer's joke was that Chanticleer is mixing up *correlation* (he crows whenever the sun rises) with *causation* (he thinks the sun rises in response to his crowing).

This sort of confusion lies at the heart of much woo thinking. If you cross your fingers before trying a difficult shot at pool and you make the shot, you're likely to attribute your success to the finger-crossing. If you miss the shot, the chances are you'll just shrug and forget it. Likewise, if you have a dream that a friend has broken his leg and the next day a friend sprains an ankle, it's very tempting to think that your dream foretold the future. You forget about all the other dreams you've had that didn't match up with any real-world events.[1] It's for very similar reasons that we think coincidences happen far more often than they do:

---

1. There's a further confusing factor when it comes to supposedly precognitive dreams: the phenomenon known as *reading back*. See page 126.

we remember the coincidences and forget about all the gazillion other events that *weren't* coincidences.

In 1977 celebrity psychic Jeane Dixon[1] predicted that the following year, 1978, would see President Jimmy Carter stand down from office, the actress Farrah Fawcett get herself a crewcut, and Pope Paul VI have a particularly dynamic year. In fact, President Carter didn't stand down, Fawcett didn't get a crewcut, and Pope Paul died. Other predictions of Dixon's that bear scrutiny are that World War III would start in 1958 and that the USSR would win the race to put a man on the moon. Her success rate was so spectacularly poor that the mathematician John Allen Paulos felt driven to coin the term "Jeane Dixon Effect" to describe instances in which vast numbers of failures or counterexamples are ignored in favor of spotlighting the few examples that serve to "prove" a wooish point.

Jeane Dixon wasn't the only professional prophet to get almost everything wrong yet have the reputation today of having been surprisingly accurate. It's impossible to assess the accuracy of Nostradamus because his supposedly prophetic quatrains (four-line verses) are so enigmatic that they're really open to any interpretation you choose to put on them. This is why no one's ever been able sensibly to *predict* anything using a Nostradamus "prophecy": it's only *afterward* that we conclude a particular piece of word salad "must have meant" a particular event. One specific prophecy that Nostradamus *did* make was of the date of his own death: November 1567.

He died on July 2, 1566.

---

1. Two US Presidents followed her psychic advice in the making of policy: Richard Nixon and Ronald Reagan.

Edgar Cayce—sometimes called the Sleeping Prophet because he prophesied (and did psychic healing, et cetera) while in a trance—was famous from the 1920s through the 1940s and still has legions of fans today who crow about how often Cayce's prophecies were spot on.

Cayce's most famous piece of prophecy came on August 13, 1941, and concerned the mainly dire events that were going to transform the planet in the period 1941–98. These included worldwide volcanic eruptions (beginning with a spectacular display by Etna), an earthquake that would destroy California, the destruction of New York and much of the rest of the eastern seaboard, the draining of the Great Lakes into the Gulf of St. Lawrence, the inundation of Japan, and, during 1968–69, the reemergence of Atlantis from beneath the waves.

Of course, 1998 has come and gone and none of these things has happened;[1] presumably diehard Cayce fans now cling to the notion that the Sleeping Prophet just got the dates wrong. At the time Cayce made the predictions, some of these might have seemed like moderately plausible bets—California slipping into the Pacific, for example. And there was much excitement in 1968 when two pilots spotted what appeared at first to be monumental architecture and roadways under the waves offshore from Bimini, Florida.

Others of Cayce's prophecies have been equal failures. When Cayce was asked in 1938 if there might be a war involving the US between 1942 and 1944, he answered that there *might* be, but only if there was insufficient desire for peace—a surmise that even the rawest political pundit

---

1. The nearest might be the tsunami that hit Japan and caused the Fukushima nuclear meltdown, but that occurred on March 11, 2011, so can hardly be claimed for the period 1941–98. Besides, the floods created by the tsunami were short-lived, not a permanent inundation.

could have made, bearing in mind that at the time Europe was pretty clearly heading toward conflict and the US was very likely to get dragged in. Among further prophecies that seem bizarrely inaccurate, even despite being couched in extraordinary vagueness, is: "When its activities are set in such a way as to bring consideration of every phase, Britain will be able to control the world for peace . . ." Well, maybe one day, but not *yet*.

In his book *Flim-Flam!* (1982) the stage magician James Randi, a celebrated debunker of charlatans, recounts a graphic example of the Jeane Dixon Effect in action. He taped an appearance by "psychic detective" Peter Hurkos on a TV chat show, and the following day listened to acquaintances commenting on Hurkos's amazing accuracy as he'd psychically revealed various bits of information about audience members. Some days later, Randi asked two of those friends to put on tape their recollections of Hurkos's performance; then he played them the recording he'd made of the performance itself.

To the friends' astonishment, and quite contrary to their recollections, Hurkos's "psychic observations" had achieved a hit rate of just 1 in 14. For the kinds of questions that were being asked—the number of children people have or whether someone close to them has a name beginning with "C"—random guesswork could be expected to produce a result at least as good as 1:14. Most professional "psychics" and stage magicians can manage far better than this thanks to a technique called cold reading.[1] So, far from being surprisingly accurate, Hurkos's performance was distinctly substandard.

---

1. A skilled cold reader can, in the course of what seems a casual conversation, pick up all sorts of information about the person they're speaking to. The key is observation—not just of how the person dresses and speaks but how they react to various remarks. If you'd like to learn how to do cold reading, there's a free downloadable PDF at http://www.skeptic.com/downloads/10_Easy_Psychic_Lessons.pdf.

Why did people misremember what they'd seen just a few days before? Why did they forget all the mistaken guesses and remember only the occasional lucky strikes? Was it just self-delusion, the satisfying of some inner need to believe in the "spiritual"? Or was it, perhaps, that the TV show *told* them to interpret what they saw as a demonstration of psychic powers and so they filtered events through that lens? Whatever the case, they certainly fell into the trap of woo thinking.

What types of woo thinking dominate the bullshitosphere today?[1] There's plenty of medical woo around, as we'll see in the next chapter, but modern woo mostly concerns mind (ESP, for example) and spirit (ghosts, prayer power, visits to Heaven, and so on). There's also a whole branch of woo thinking that associates natural phenomena like tornadoes and earthquakes with God's wrath—or, rather, with whatever makes the woo thinker wrathful, whether it be gay marriage or racial integration. Pat Robertson and Jerry Falwell attributed the 9/11 terrorist attacks and the 2005 flooding of New Orleans by Hurricane Katrina to God's fury about sexual permissiveness and the widespread toleration of homosexuality, while Rush Limbaugh set some sort of bullshittery record when he theorized that the spectacular 2010 eruption of the Icelandic volcano Eyjafjallajökull might be God registering His objection to Obamacare.

Our national discourse contains far too much woo thinking for us to be able to cover in this book, so we'll just have to content ourselves with a few examples.

---

1. It's tempting to reply, "All of them."

THERAPEUTIC PRAYER

Lots of people will tell you that prayer has therapeutic power—that it can help people who're sick get better faster. We've already seen (page 112) the tragic consequences this bit of woo belief can have.

Nearly a century and a half ago, Francis Galton (whom we met briefly in connection with eugenics) published a paper called "Statistical Inquiries into the Efficacy of Prayer" (1872). He had the very simple idea of comparing the life expectancies of men in various different professions. (Left out of consideration were the lower classes, whose life expectancies were, as now, much shorter due to malnutrition, lack of hygiene, and lack of medical care; and women, because at the time women didn't have professions.) It was immediately obvious that members of the clergy, whom one can assume were prayed for a lot, did little better than, say, lawyers, prayers about whom might be expected to have a life-*shortening* effect!

Worst of all fared members of the royal family, despite churches habitually calling on their flocks to pray for reigning monarchs and their kin.

Needless to say, Galton's essay provoked considerable controversy, with the devout protesting loudly about his conclusions, his tone, and his lack of "respect" for their beliefs. What almost all of Galton's critics failed to do, of course, was confront his statistics, which spoke for themselves.

In 1996, the views of nearly three hundred physicians attending the annual meeting of the American Academy of Family Physicians were canvassed on the subject of therapeutic prayer. It turned out that 75 percent of them thought a patient's recovery could be aided by the prayers of others and a whopping 99 percent thought religious beliefs had the power to heal.

What scientific evidence, if any, do we have for therapeutic prayer as a genuine phenomenon? Probably the most-cited paper on the subject has been "Does Prayer Influence the Success of In Vitro Fertilization–Embryo Transfer?" (2001) by Kwang Y. Cha, Rogerio A. Lobo, and Daniel P. Wirth. In this study, 199 women who sought *in vitro* fertilization were divided into two groups. Photographs of the women in the first group were distributed to Christians in the US, Canada, and Australia, who prayed for the women's successful fertilization. The other women formed a control group; while they may have been prayed for by friends and relatives, they weren't being subjected to the same anonymous prayer bombardment. None of the women knew there was an experiment under way.

The reported results were startling. The success rate for *in vitro* fertilizations is ordinarily about 25 percent, and this was the rate shown in the control group. However, the rate among the beneficiaries of the international prayer campaign was far higher, at about 50 percent.

Many scientists were unconvinced. For one thing, it was worrying that one of the study's three authors, Wirth, had published extensively on the paranormal, in which it was only too evident he was a believer. He gave his affiliation here and in other articles as Healing Sciences Research International, of which he was the head and which it was later discovered seemed to consist of little more than a PO box.

Among the skeptics was Professor Bruce L. Flamm of the University of California, Irvine, Medical Center. Flamm wrote a three-part critique of the paper, questioning its methodology and its conclusions. Meanwhile, Lobo was beginning to have second thoughts, now saying that, even though listed as the paper's lead author, he hadn't participated in the study but merely provided "editorial assistance"; in due course, he asked that his name be removed. Also, in 2002, co-author Wirth was indicted for mail and bank fraud, eventually pleading guilty in April 2004. The paper is now regarded as at best unreliable.

Another study of therapeutic prayer was done by Mitchell Krucoff and his colleagues and published in the *American Heart Journal* in 2001. The researchers arranged for one group of patients to be prayed for, without their knowledge and by people they didn't know, and for another group to serve as an unprayed-for control. Krucoff, a cardiologist at Duke Clinical Research Institute, Durham, NC, made some startling claims in the media about the study's results. In an article in the August 2000 issue of *Hippocrates*[1] he said:

> Adverse outcomes in the prayer group were 50 percent
> to 100 percent fewer than in the standard therapy group.
> In the patients who received any of the noetic therapies,[2]
> including prayer, we found a 30 percent reduction for
> every adverse outcome we measured.

The only trouble was that these claims weren't supported by the published study. Just for a start, although all of the unprayed-for people had survived, one of the prayed-for patients had died. *That* was surely an "adverse outcome" that hadn't been reduced by 30 percent! Overall, it seemed the praying had made no difference at all.

---

1. Published by the Massachusetts Medical Society.
2. He's using the word "noetic" to mean, basically, "spiritual."

This episode might be marked off as just an excited scientist over-stating his case were it not for the impact Krucoff's public claims had on the beliefs of the public. Conduct a quick Google search and you'll soon find yourself looking at countless citations of either this paper or its 2005 follow-up (which again found no evidence of prayer's medical effectiveness) in support of some or another blogger's contention that prayer really does have therapeutic benefit. Of course, those bloggers would probably make the claim anyway, but Krucoff's PR campaign gave the woo-mongers what can look like some genuine scientific support.

The John Templeton Foundation is an organization that tries to reconcile religion and science. It has funded a couple of studies of therapeutic prayer. The first was done by a group headed by cardiologist Herbert Benson of the Mind/Body Medical Institute in Massachusetts and was published in *American Heart Journal* in April 2006. Benson and his colleagues tracked over 1,800 patients recovering from heart surgery for more than a decade.

They concluded that prayers by strangers unknown to the patient had zero effect on the patient's recovery—essentially what Krucoff's papers had indicated.

Startlingly, though, in cases where patients *knew* they were being prayed for, there was an apparent *negative* link between patient welfare and prayer: The patients were actually more likely to suffer complications! Benson and his colleagues suspected knowledge of the prayer might be making some of these patients overoptimistic about how quickly they were recovering, so that they did foolish things.

The Templeton Foundation funded a second study that produced what seemed more favorable results, but this research has so much wrong with its methodology that it's hard to take seriously. The biologist P. Z. Myers posted a useful analysis—"Templeton Prayer Study Meets Expectations"—on his blog *Pharyngula* in August 2010. One of the conclusions of the new team seemed to be that its results differed from those found by Benson and his colleagues because the latter were using *the wrong sort of prayer*!

Alarmingly, a credulous account of the second study was soon (in August 5, 2010) posted on the US Government's website: "Can Hands-On Prayer Help Heal?" by Amanda Gardner. This article also called on the opinion of an "integrative-medicine practitioner" called J. Adam Rindfleisch. "There's a lot out there about the power of touch and human connection and just being present with somebody, and whether that might be contributing to healing," he opined. "It stands to reason if someone is near you and you know they're caring about you and want your well being, you're more likely to [get better]."

Stands to reason? Benson's study had already shown it didn't "stand to reason" at all!

It seems the efficacy of therapeutic prayer is not something amenable to scientific analysis: if the research shows there's no effect, then obviously it's the research that must be wrong. There *is* good evidence that prayer can offer minor health benefits . . . for the person doing the praying. As with meditation, the act of praying triggers the relaxation response: metabolic and heart rates decrease, the immune system is bolstered, et cetera. But this is not what is generally meant by the term "therapeutic prayer."

SCIENCE INVESTIGATES

Scientific attempts to investigate the paranormal really got under way in the nineteenth century because of the huge popularity of Spiritualism.

In 1848 in Hydesville, New York, the two sisters Kate and Margaret Fox, aged 12 and 15, were at the center of what seemed like an outbreak of very spooky activity in their home: strange rapping noises, unearthly creakings, and more. The whole neighborhood was fascinated by the doings in the Fox home. The sisters developed a code whereby they could communicate with the spirit who was haunting their house, and everything took off from there. Soon people all over the country, as well as in the UK and Europe, were claiming they could communicate with the dead, and a whole new profession was born: spirit medium.

Toward the ends of their lives, Kate and Margaret confessed the affair had been a hoax, and demonstrated how the tricks were done, but their confession went almost entirely ignored. Ever since Spiritualism began and mediums have repeatedly been caught faking, this same reasoning has appeared:

- Just because Medium A is a faker doesn't mean anybody else is.
- It doesn't even mean that Medium A is a total cheat, because it could be she was cheating *just this once* and is genuinely communicating with the dead all the rest of the time!

Yeah, right.

The Society for Psychical Research (SPR) was founded in the UK in 1882 in an attempt to investigate scientifically the widespread "psychic phenomena" that were all the rage; it still exists today. A Scottish branch of the SPR was founded as recently as 1987 by the Glasgow University astronomer Archie Roy. Of considerably greater antiquity than the Scottish branch is the American Society for Psychical Research (ASPR), founded in 1885, just three years after its UK counterpart; among its founders there was the famous psychologist William James, and one of its benefactors was Chester Carlson, inventor of the xerox. The ASPR's first president was the astronomer Simon Newcomb.[1] Other countries had their own equivalents.

Don't get the idea that the SPR's founders were just gullible crackpots. At the time the subject of the psychic—life after death, communication with spirits, clairvoyance, precognition, and all the rest—seemed something that merited urgent scientific inquiry. Among the organization's early presidents were Arthur Balfour (later UK Prime Minister), and the scientists William James (the same man who helped found the ASPR), Sir William Crookes, Sir Oliver Lodge, Charles Robert Richet, and even the Nobel Prize-winning physicist Lord Rayleigh.[2] Right up until more recent times, some quite highly regarded scientists have served as SPR presidents.

---

1. Elsewhere Simon Newcomb expressed extremely cautious views about the potential of science and technology, with comments like "Flight by machines heavier than air is unpractical and insignificant, if not utterly impossible" and "We are probably nearing the limit of all we can know about astronomy." Yet he happily countenanced the notion of communicating with the dead!

2. Among Rayleigh's long list of achievements was the discovery (with William Ramsey) of the gas argon and the explanation (Rayleigh scattering) of why the sky looks blue.

Spiritualists were not unnaturally nervous of the SPR. The tools and attitudes of science obviously represented a threat. Although there are countless examples in the SPR's records of even the most distinguished scientific investigators having the wool pulled over their eyes by fraudulent mediums, there are also plenty of cases in which their ingenuity and industry exposed those frauds. They also made some contributions to mainstream psychology. It was, for example, SPR researchers, not orthodox psychologists, who first described the phenomenon of "reading back." Through their understanding of how we "read back" our dreams—if we later come across something that's vaguely reminiscent of a dream, we tend to remodel our memories of the dream to make the fit seem exact—the researchers were able to show that scads of "psychic dream" cases could be quite easily explained.

There was also a religious motive for the founding of the SPR. Recent advances in science had left less and less room for the spiritual in explanations of the world. At least some of the SPR's early stalwarts hoped the "science" they were undertaking would confirm there was something spiritual still there to which they might cling. In 1880, one of those founders, Henry Sidgwick, wrote: "*Either* one must believe in ghosts, modern miracles, et cetera, *or* there can be no ground for giving credence to the Gospel story." It's probably not a line of reasoning many would follow today.

During the first couple of decades of the twentieth century, it became obvious that the vast majority of professional spirit mediums were basically frauds out to fleece the gullible—parasites on other people's grief. Among those most active in exposing fraudulent spirit mediums was the famous conjurer and escapologist Harry Houdini. He was part of the panel hired by the magazine *Scientific American* to investigate mediums competing for the hefty cash prize it was offering to anyone who could prove their "psychic gifts" were genuine. Houdini's knowledge of conjuring tricks was invaluable in stopping the mediums from doing things that the other researchers would have believed impossible. A modern equivalent of Houdini is the conjurer James "The Amazing" Randi, who, as we'll see in a moment, is likewise adept at exposing the tricks of "psychically gifted" frauds.

Because of the activities of Houdini and others, "psychic research" became a bit of a joke—phony ectoplasm, trumpet-blowing spirits, mediums with gadgets stuffed in their underwear, et cetera. In the early 1930s, the US researcher J. B. Rhine therefore devised the term *extra-sensory* (or *extra-sensory*) *perception* (ESP) to cover the supposed "sixth sense" abilities: telepathy, clairvoyance, and precognition.[1] At about the same time, Rhine and his wife and colleague Louisa adopted from the German researcher Max Dessoir the word *parapsychology* to describe the "science" of researching ESP and related abilities.

Rhine's research—done at Duke University in Durham, North Carolina, where he established the Parapsychology Laboratory[2]—supposedly gave parapsychology a whole new respectability, yet it became apparent that what had so bedeviled the endeavors of the SPR was still a major problem: people cheat, and those supposed to investigate them are all too easily bamboozled. There are a couple of fundamental principles that Rhine and many of his successors failed to observe:

---

1. In fact, as early as the 1920s the German researchers Gustav Pagenstecher and Rudolph Tischner were using the term *aussersinnliche Wahrehmung*; this translates as "extrasensory perception."

2. He also founded the Parapsychological Association, the Foundation for Research on the Nature of Man (the germ of what's now known as the Rhine Research Center and Institute for Parapsychology), and a peer-reviewed journal, *The Journal of Parapsychology*.

- Always check to see if a phenomenon can be explained without recourse to "special powers" or the supernatural. The mundane explanation you come up with may not turn out to be the correct one, but *the very fact that it exists* means the phenomenon isn't proof of the supernatural. If two people seem to be communicating telepathically, remember that "mentalist" stage acts have for well over a century tricked even highly intelligent, skeptical audiences into thinking the performers are telepathic. (That's why stage magicians like Houdini and Randi are so invaluable in parapsychology!)

- Extraordinary claims require extraordinary evidence, as the astronomer Carl Sagan was fond of saying. What he meant was that, if you claim something (e.g., telepathy) exists that would involve rewriting whole tranches of firmly established science, then you need mountains of pretty convincing evidence before your claim has to be taken seriously.[1]

Between the 1930s and 1960s, many of the public and the media did take Rhine's work seriously, but the interest of other scientists tailed off fairly rapidly when no one else could replicate his results: when they tried to repeat his experiments they failed to find the evidence he said he'd found. Furthermore, it emerged that he'd made various errors in

---

1. Also, as Christopher Hitchens remarked, "That which can be asserted without evidence can be dismissed without evidence."

designing his experiments, most notably that he'd left the door wide open for cheats; it seems never to have occurred to him that his experimental subjects might be dishonest. When Rhine died in 1980, it was as if his influence died with him.

The Committee for the Scientific Investigation of Claims of the Paranormal (CSICOP) was founded in 1976. It had been kick-started some months earlier by a statement called "Objections to Astrology" published in *The Humanist* for September/October 1975. Then as now, responsible scientists were alarmed by the sheer volume of bullshit being foisted upon the public by the US media. Signed by 186 leading scientists, including 18 Nobel laureates, the statement read in part:

> One would imagine, in this day of widespread enlightenment and education, that it would be unnecessary to debunk beliefs based on magic and superstition. Yet, acceptance of astrology pervades modern society. We are especially disturbed by the continued uncritical dissemination of astrological charts, forecasts, and horoscopes by the media and by otherwise reputable newspapers, magazines, and book publishers. This can only contribute to the growth of irrationalism and obscurantism.

The name CSICOP can of course be read as a pun for "psi cop," but apparently this was an accident. In 2006 CSICOP became the Committee for Skeptical Inquiry (CSI).

Where the SPR and Rhine had assumed they were investigating something that actually existed—that the paranormal/supernatural is real even if hard to pin down—the position of CSICOP/CSI is that the paranormal/supernatural almost certainly *doesn't* exist, and that the organization's job is to investigate reported occurrences with a view to offering a rational explanation. Naturally this has brought a great deal of criticism in its direction, and not only from people who've been themselves comprehensively debunked or seen their pet hypotheses shredded. Even some skeptics have suggested that CSI runs the risk of throwing the baby out with the bathwater in its demolition of woo. Certainly, if you're accustomed to the vapidities of the commercial broadcast media, reading a copy of the CSI's bimonthly journal, *Skeptical Inquirer*, can be quite startling—or, as some might say, invigorating.

CHEATING PSYCHICS

In 1983 James Randi held a press conference in New York at which he revealed an extensive hoax that he'd perpetrated with the aid of two fellow-conjurers, Michael Edwards and Steven Shaw. Randi had sent the two young men to the McDonnell Laboratory for Psychic Research, set up in 1979 at Washington University, St Louis, using a $500,000 grant donated by James McDonnell of the McDonnell Douglas Corporation.

There they had stunned the resident parapsychological investigators, led by physicist Peter Phillips, with some astonishing demonstrations of psychokinesis, spoonbending, et cetera—all achieved by, of course, trickery. Randi had even gone so far as to send Phillips warnings that he and his researchers were being bamboozled by the pair, but Phillips had done little of any effectiveness to check their backgrounds or tighten controls on the relevant experiments.

The McDonnell Laboratory never recovered its reputation, and in 1985 it closed. Although a few woo-mongers expressed outrage that Randi should have pulled such a "despicable" stunt, most reputable parapsychologists (Phillips eventually included) seemed grateful, regarding this as a salutary lesson—a long-needed kick in the pants for shoddy or credulous researchers.

And there was a further message, this one for the mainstream scientific community: When investigating paranormal claims, mainstream scientists are perhaps the worst researchers of all. The reason's obvious. Science is not really geared to take account of cheating: Evidence may be ambiguous and hard to interpret, but it's not usually faked.

Randi and his youthful colleagues were telling scientists that, if they wanted to investigate the paranormal—riddled with conmen and charlatans as it always has been—they should unfailingly include a professional conjurer as part of their team. It was the same lesson learned decades earlier, when distinguished scientists were fooled by Spiritualist charlatans whom Harry Houdini deftly exposed, but it had been forgotten.

To take a single example of how easy it is to cheat a scientist in standard ESP experiments: The psychologist George Estabrooks once designed a telepathy experiment that he believed completely hoax-proof. Two people were placed in separate rooms. One person would turn up the cards in a deck and attempt to transmit telepathically the color (red or black) of each newly exposed card. Two friends of Estabrooks volunteered to show him what was wrong with the experiment. When they became the experimental subjects,, the "percipient" (the supposed receiver of the telepathic message) scored 52 out of 52.

Estabrooks could find no evidence of cheating or detect any complicity between the two, yet the trick was simplicity itself. The two had agreed beforehand that the "percipient" would assume, unless it were indicated otherwise, that the first, third, fifth, et cetera, cards turned up were red and the even-numbered cards were black. Should an odd-numbered card be black or an even-numbered card be red, the "sender" would clear his throat, scrape his chair, drum his fingers, or otherwise make a noise. Had the friends attempted to perpetuate their ruse for several decks of cards rather than just one, Estabrooks would presumably have cottoned on—there's only so often you can plausibly clear your throat!—but over this single run the trick was impenetrable to him. A good conjurer, by contrast, would have spotted it at once.

SPELLING ERRORS IN THE STARS

You probably know someone who checks their horoscope in the paper every day, and who's frequently surprised by how astonishingly accurate the comments of Mystick Matilda or Strabismus the Seer can be. To someone who doesn't believe in astrology, it's easy to spot the trick: if a comment is vague enough that it can be applied to just about anyone, plenty of readers will think it applies to *them*:

- "You'll experience moments of self-doubt today." Well, most of us are likely to, *especially if we've been told we're going to.*
- "An old friend or family member will be on your mind." Again a good bet, especially if you've been told so in advance.

NOSTRADAMUS AND WORLD WAR TWO

It would be a kindness to call Nostradamus's predictions ambiguous: "incomprehensible" is a better term. They're open to so many alternative interpretations that during World War II both sides saw fit to use them as a propaganda tool.

The first use was by the Nazis, inspired by Goebbels—or, rather, by Goebbels's wife, who'd chosen Nostradamus as her bedtime reading. It didn't take Goebbels's nimble mind long to realize that appropriate verses could be presented as if to describe a complete German triumph. Doctored copies were accordingly airdropped into France in May 1940. It's not clear how much good this escapade did the Nazis, but it was imitated by the Allies, who later during the conflict dropped their own doctored version of the prophecies onto German cities.

- "You are generous to a fault. Be careful you do not allow unscrupulous people around you to take advantage of your goodheartedness." Who among us doesn't warm to flattery? And, if we're not in fact generous at all, we're almost certainly suspicious that people around us are trying to rip us off.
- "You will receive a message from a major Hollywood studio telling you they'd like you to star in a new movie opposite George Clooney." Of course, news-

paper astrologers can never make a specific prediction like this, not just because the chances of its coming true are virtually zero but because it'd have to come true for one in every twelve of their readers—every Sagittarius, or every Capricorn, for example.

Professional astrologers operate at a far higher level of sophistication than their newspaper counterparts, and some quite genuinely believe in what they're doing. If you consult a real astrologer they'll draw up a chart (a birth chart or natal chart) showing the positions of the stars, planets, sun, and moon in the sky at the moment of your birth, then calculate the supposed influences these celestial bodies would have had on you. From those calculations the astrologer produces a profile of you.

Leaving aside any questions of *how* the positions of the stars and planets could have any influence on you, how meaningful are these charts?

In the early 1980s, a team led by Shawn Carlson at the University of California in Berkeley decided to test this. They conducted a large-scale experiment (reported in *Nature* in 1985) in which astrologers were asked to match individuals to profiles drawn up using natal charts as well as to others that were created using something grandly called the California Psychological (or Personality) Inventory; this involved the individuals filling in a questionnaire, their profile being drawn up on the basis of their answers.

As well as the astrologers trying to match the profiles to the individuals, the individuals *themselves* tried to identify their own profiles from among sets of others.

FREUD FINDS EVIDENCE OF TELEPATHY?

Sigmund Freud, the "father" of psychoanalysis, was less convinced about ESP than the other great psychoanalytic pioneer, his student Carl Gustav Jung. But he did mention a few cases he thought might be persuasive.

In one, a childless wife was told by a fortune teller she would have two children by the time she was 32. In fact, she didn't. However, her *mother* had borne two children by the time she was 32 and it was this, Freud deemed, that the fortune teller had telepathically detected. Freud triumphantly diagnosed that the daughter must have had incestuous yearnings for her father, and thus identified with her mother—hence the fortune teller's telepathic confusion of the two women.

How many women bear two children by the time they're 32? The answer is of course: Lots. It's difficult to work out why Freud thought telepathy (or those incestuous yearnings) should have been involved at all!

You'll probably not be surprised to learn that the astrologers didn't score significantly better than chance. But, interestingly, *neither did the individuals*! Confronted by a genuine, in-depth psychological profile of themselves, they had difficulty recognizing it.

What better confirmation could there be that it's open to an astrologer to present almost random profiles? So long as they don't go too far into specifics, the vast majority of customers will be impressed by how accurate those profiles are.

WOO BARB

Channeling is the supposed paranormal ability to pick up a psychic message; for example, a Spiritualist medium channels messages from the dead.

It's hard to know what to make of the case of Barbara Bell, of San Anselmo, California, who believed she could channel Barbie—that's right, the plastic doll whose boyfriend is Ken. "Since childhood I have been gifted with an intensely personal, growth-oriented relationship with Barbie, the polyethylene essence who is 700 million teaching essences," she explained. "Her truths are too important to be prepackaged. My sincere hope is to let the voice of Barbie, my inner nametwin [*sic*], come through. Barbie's messages are offered in love." Accordingly, in 1992 Bell founded the *Barbie Channeling Newsletter*, where various mysteries were unveiled to folks in quest of arcane wisdom. Apparently Barbie's first channeled message for us all was: "I need respect."

Alas, Mattel, the manufacturers of the Barbie doll, took a dim view and in 1994 issued a cease-and-desist letter to stop the two Barbies in their tracks.

Carlson's results echoed those from a pair of far earlier experiments done by the French psychologist Michel Gauquelin.[1] Under pseudonyms, he submitted the birth charts of ten convicted murderers to a

---

1. Some of Gauquelin's other work is generally regarded as favorable to astrology, so he's widely cited in pro-astrology texts.

commercial astrologer, requesting horoscopes. The profiles the astrologer drew up revealed no psychopathic tendencies, just humdrum stuff. Then Gauquelin put advertisements in the newspaper offering free horoscopes to anyone who wrote in asking for them. Many people did, and to each he sent, pretending it was theirs, a copy of a profile drawn up astrologically according to the birth chart of a notorious serial killer. Of those people who responded, the vast majority congratulated him on the accuracy of their profile!

MALAYSIA AIRLINES FLIGHT 370

On March 8, 2014, Malaysia Airlines Flight 370 took off from Kuala Lumpur International Airport, bound for Beijing. Within an hour after takeoff the plane lost contact with air traffic control. Radar tracking showed that thereafter there was at least one deliberate course change before the plane was lost altogether. Over the ensuing weeks, a vast international search was mounted.

Meanwhile, even though commercial pilots offered perfectly rational explanations for everything that had been observed, conspiracy theorists had a field day. Could one of the pilots have gone mad and hijacked his own plane to North Korea? Had Flight 370 been taken over by terrorists? Could all this be related to the crisis in the Ukraine, which was going on at the same time? CNN's coverage of the missing airplane crowded out its reports on that crisis—and on everything else of importance.

And the woo crowd went wild. The Malaysian government enlisted shamans to use ritual magic in an attempt to aid the search. Why oh why, wailed the bullshitosphere, were the news media failing even to mention the possibilities of freak wormholes or alien abductions? Could the mystery be related to the legendary disappearances in the Bermuda Triangle?[1] Pop star Courtney Love posted a photo to Facebook which, she claimed, showed an oil slick and wreckage. CNN presenter Don Lemon, interviewing Brad Meltzer of the "mystery"/conspiracy theory TV show *Decoded*, suggested that perhaps in this instance a mere conspiracy theory wasn't enough and we should be discussing supernatural explanations: "People are saying to me, why aren't you talking about the possibility—and I'm just putting it out there—that something odd happened to this plane, something beyond our understanding?" A few days later he asked former US Department of Transportation Inspector General Mary Schiavo about the possibility of Flight 370 having been swallowed by a black hole. "I know it's preposterous," he qualified.

CNN Headline News guest host Lynn Berry went further, calling on professional self-professed psychic Lisa Williams for advice. According to the webzine *Mediaite*, reporting on March 21, 2014, Williams claimed she knew some of the passengers were still alive "and are being held in an undisclosed location" where apparently there were lots of trees. The magazine's report continued: "Williams said she was just informed by the voices in her 'witchy woo land' that the mystery behind the plane's disappearance will be finally resolved 'within the next three weeks.'" Of course, very much longer than three weeks has gone

---

1. The Bermuda Triangle is an area, defined by Bermuda, Puerto Rico, and the Florida coast, where (supposedly) ships and aircraft are lost so frequently that the only possible explanation must be a supernatural one. In *The Bermuda Triangle Mystery—Solved* (1976) researcher Larry Kusche went through those cases one by one and showed there were viable non-supernatural explanations for all of them, and that the Bermuda Triangle was no more dangerous than you'd expect such a region to be.

by and still (November 2014) there has been no trace discovered of the missing plane and no solution to "the mystery behind the plane's disappearance." The claim about some of the passengers still being alive is especially cruel to people hoping against hope that it might be true, that their loved ones might indeed have survived, only to have those hopes dashed again.

And, to cap it all, Uri Geller announced he'd been called in. Just what everyone needed: a bent aircraft.

$$\oslash$$

3. BUGS AND BODIES: MYSTERIES OF MEDICINE

In 1990, an episode of the CBS show *Face to Face with Connie Chung* was dedicated to silicone-gel breast implants.

These implants, invented in 1961 by a pair of Texas surgeons, had allowed millions of women to artificially enlarge their breasts. In the vast majority of cases, the surgery had gone well and the women were happy with the outcome. In a few, though, there had been complications and some of the recipients complained they'd started to suffer various symptoms. In the 1980s, the Public Citizen Health Research Group, a Ralph Nader organization, suggested leaky implants might cause cancer, but there was zero evidence and the idea faded away. In 1984, Maria Stern won a case for damages against the implant manufacturer Dow Corning on the basis of extremely dubious court evidence that her implants *could* have been responsible for her systemic autoimmune disease.

However, so far as medical science could establish, there was no real danger from the operation or the implants. Even so, in 1982, the Food and Drug Administration (FDA) decided caution was advisable and that the implant manufacturers—foremost among them Dow Corning—should be asked to demonstrate, through clinical trials or otherwise, that the implants were safe.

Dow Corning and the others seem not to have taken this seriously, even when, a few years later, the FDA gave them a deadline of June 1988 to supply the evidence. In 1992 the head of the FDA, David

Kessler, put his foot down and halted the sale of the implants until the requisite evidence was forthcoming.

One reason for his impatience was that episode of *Face to Face with Connie Chung*. Chung is a very likable broadcaster, so viewers tended to feel with her as she interviewed a succession of women who'd suffered devastating illnesses since receiving breast implants. Any viewer would have concluded, judging on face value alone—which is unfortunately how most television watchers *do* judge information—that silicone-gel breast implants were killers, or nearabouts, and that the manufacturers were engaging in a massive coverup to conceal this unpalatable piece of information from the public.

The trouble is, of course, that—as we've noted before—correlation doesn't necessarily imply causation. If I eat porridge for breakfast and then start sneezing later in the day, it doesn't mean it was the porridge that gave me the cold. Scientists are well aware of the danger of mistaking correlation for causation, but the legal system isn't, and so for years after Kessler's temporary ban there was an epidemic of lawsuits against the manufacturers, with huge damages often awarded on the basis of scientific evidence that was shaky, nonsensical, or even, in some instances, outright fraudulent.

Scientific researchers and science journalists who spoke out against this bullshit were often subject to persecution. Sherine Gabriel, the lead author of the first paper to set out the evidence that silicone-gel implants were completely safe, found herself served with subpoenas demanding all sorts of confidential information about the volunteers who'd taken part in the clinical trials she'd run. She wasn't the only one. Producing this and the other information demanded would not only have tied her up for months or years but would have been in breach of the contracts of confidentiality she had with the volunteers.

These subpoenas came from the lawyers who'd been making a fat living out of the implant cases. They had no scientific basis—or indeed any rational basis at all. Their sole purpose was to harass. It's a pattern we come across again and again when lawyers and politicians don't like scientific evidence.

By the mid-1990s, about twenty studies had shown that silicone-gel implants were safe. Various relevant scientific organizations—like the American Medical Association (AMA)—had issued statements to the same effect. Sanity finally reached the courts (in this respect at least!), with judges beginning to kick out the frivolous damages claims.

Of course, the manufacturers didn't get back all the money they'd had to pay out on the basis of bogus medical claims. In fact, when Dow Corning went bankrupt in 1998, it had to find $3.2 billion to pay toward the damages that had been awarded against the company on grounds that were by then known to be spurious.

There's plenty of it about in the medical world—and no wonder. If your phone goes wrong it's a nuisance but (probably) not the end of the world. If your body goes wrong it very well *could* be the end of the world, at least so far as you're concerned. It's hardly surprising, then, that people get frightened for their health, and so are vulnerable to believing all kinds of bullshit.

ALTERNATIVE MEDICINE

Really there's no such thing as alternative medicine. If something works, it becomes part of mainstream, scientific medicine. And if it *doesn't* work, it isn't medicine.

It's partly for this reason that some people prefer the term *complementary medicine*, as if scientific and unscientific medicine somehow work hand-in-hand. A quite different set of people prefer the term *quack medicine*. There's also *traditional medicine*, referring to the therapies that have been around for centuries. One measure of the difference in efficacy between traditional and scientific medicine is that in 1800 most people in the developed world died before reaching the age of 30, whatever the old saws said about "three score years and ten"; today average life expectancy is nearly 80.

Of course, other factors have played a part in that astonishing change, but the advance of scientific medicine has been a very significant contributor.

Embarrassingly, some European governments, including those of the UK, Switzerland, France, and Germany, give credence to and/or waste taxpayer money on these non-scientific therapies, while in the US the National Institutes of Health, supposedly dedicated to medical science, is lumbered with the National Center for Complementary and Alternative Medicine (NCCAM), whose website includes articles that are for the most part perfectly sensible—like "Review of Research Shows, Overall, Acupuncture Did Not Increase Pregnancy Rates with IVF" (July 2013)—except that effort and our tax dollars have been expended demonstrating a result we could already have guessed.

Why do people think alternative medicine works? There are various reasons.

For example, sometimes traditional therapies, at least, *do* work. For centuries, herbalists used the foxglove plant (*Digitalis* species) for various illnesses. Although the symptoms they treated were somewhat scattershot, in some instances the treatments were effective. The main problem was that foxgloves are poisonous, so if you got the dosage wrong you could end up with a dead patient. Eventually science analyzed foxgloves to find out the active principle, to determine exactly which conditions it was good for, and to establish safe dosages. Today, people with certain heart conditions—atrial fibrillation is one—can be prescribed digitalis (digoxin), which is the same stuff as in foxgloves but uncontaminated and in a precisely measured dose.

That point about the "precisely measured dose" is important. It's one reason why scientific medicine is more effective than other forms.

Some other herbal medicines have been discovered to be genuinely useful, and the substances concerned are now a part of modern medicine's toolkit. A major example is aspirin, or salicylic acid. It's the active ingredient in the willow bark that has been used as a painkiller since ancient times.

A second reason why some people swear by one alternative therapy or another is the *placebo effect*. Researchers have found that, when people are sick, some of them will show improvement if they *think* they're getting a medical treatment even if what they're being given is a fake (a placebo)—a pill made of sugar rather than a drug, for example. No one knows for sure why this happens. Maybe it's often just that being given some medicine cheers you up because you assume you're soon going to stop feeling lousy. And it's not just in a few cases that the placebo effect works, either. When clinical trials are being done on new drugs, researchers generally reckon that about 30 percent of the people getting the drug would show improvement anyway because of the placebo effect.

This means that any alternative therapist can expect to get good results about 30 percent of the time.[1] That's quite enough for stories of their successes to be circulated widely, and to make other people believe the quack therapy works.

There's also a reporting bias in operation. If someone's cancer goes into remission not long after they were treated with Dr. Wonderful's Patented Magic Dungballs™, the story's all over the internet in about three seconds flat. If someone dies of their cancer not long after they took Dr. Wonderful's Patented Magic Dungballs™, where's the story in that? You never hear about it.

That leads us to a third reason why people think alternative therapies work. Back on page 58, we saw that "the plural of "anecdote" is not "evidence"—in other words, a whole lot of unproved bits of information don't add up to a proof. You can find anecdotes all over the place about people being cured by homeopathy or color therapy or acupuncture or any of the other alternative therapies. When those therapies are tried out under experimental conditions, however, the results are very different.

---

1. Many mainstream doctors admit that often the prescriptions they write for patients are just placebos. Sometimes patients demand pills they've seen advertised on TV and the doctors prescribe them knowing that many patients will feel better simply because they believed the TV ad. An odd further factor is that expensive placebos get higher success rate than cheaper ones, and that injected placebos work better than pills or liquids. There are recorded instances of military surgeons, lacking anesthetics, injecting patients with (harmless) salt water and finding this did the job just as well.

Finally, it's worth remembering that we tend consistently to underestimate how good our body is at repairing itself. Even in epidemics of truly lethal diseases like bubonic plague, there are some people whose bodies will reject the bacillus and others who, although stricken, will recover without any medical attention at all.

Here we're going to look at just a couple of the most popular alternative therapies.

HOMEOPATHY

What's often difficult for us to realize is quite how recent of a science medicine is. For example, while the idea that some diseases are infectious seems obvious to us, it wasn't as obvious to our ancestors: One reason epidemics spread so swiftly through ancient Rome was that the Roman doctors often prescribed sick people a trip (or series of trips) to the public baths—where, of course, they mixed intimately with everyone else. Again, the notion that illness—especially mental illness—was a consequence of people being invaded by demons lasted for many centuries (and can still be found in some communities today).

Another idea that lasted a long time was the four humors. Ancient Greek philosophers like Aristotle had concluded that everything was made up of just four elements: earth, air, fire, and water. In medieval Europe, it was thought the human body was governed by four humors, corresponding to those four elements:

- black bile/melancholy, corresponding to earth
- yellow bile/choler, corresponding to air

- blood, corresponding to fire
- phlegm, corresponding to water[1]

Illness was what happened when the four humors fell out of balance in your body, and the job of the physician was to try to get them back into kilter. For example, if you were hot (fiery) from a fever, then it would be a good idea to lose some blood, so the physician would open up a blood vessel until you'd lost a pint or two.

This form of medicine was known as *enantiopathy* (you were trying to cure a symptom by applying something that would cause its opposite) or *allopathy* (you were trying to cure a symptom by applying something that would cause a different symptom). Unsurprisingly, even the placebo effect didn't come to the rescue of a lot of the luckless patients.[2]

The word *homeopathy* refers to a form of medicine in which you try to treat a symptom by applying something that would cause the *same* symptom. It was the brainchild of a German physician called Christian Friedrich Samuel Hahnemann, who was active in the late eighteenth century and the first part of the nineteenth. He saw that the failure rate of contemporary medicine was astonishingly high and concluded this was because physicians misunderstood what symptoms were: They thought symptoms were a product of the illness, whereas Hahnemann suggested they were manifestations of the body *coping with* the disease.[3]

---

1. In a sense, the idea of four humors is still with us. Even today we talk about people being "melancholic" or "choleric" or "sanguine" or "phlegmatic" or "bilious."

2. The practice of bleeding was surprisingly long-lived, still being common in the western world until the late nineteenth century. Sometimes the bloodletting was done using leeches: the physician attached a few of these bloodsuckers to the patient and let them engorge themselves.

3. In many instances he was absolutely correct. If you have a fever, for example, that's because your body's immune system is fighting the infection.

So Hahnemann's big idea was that the way to cure illness was not to counter the symptoms but to help them. Instead of applying something that would have the opposite effect to the symptom (throwing iced water over someone with a fever, for example), he suggested using medicines that would have the same effect as the symptom. However, Hahnemann was conscious that increasing a symptom could be dangerous in itself, so he said the dosages in his medicines should be very small.

Extremely small.

Um, smaller even than that.

Hahnemann decreed that his medicines should be diluted several times, the mixture being given a prescribed number of shakes between each dilution. The overall result is that most homeopathic medicines are so dilute that there's *not a single molecule* of the supposed active ingredient left in the dose. In some cases the dose could be the size of all the world's oceans and there *still* wouldn't be a relevant molecule in it.

Even if somehow you managed to beat the impossible odds and be so lucky as to have that single molecule of the active ingredient in your dose, what effect can a single molecule have on your body? Just in the same way that a single molecule of strychnine can't do you any harm, a single molecule of medicine can't do you any good.

Of course, Hahnemann couldn't have been aware of this as a problem, since no one knew about molecules at the time.[1] Modern fans of homeopathy, however, obviously *are* aware of the dilution conundrum.

---

1. It was his contemporary, John Dalton, who first formulated the modern atomic theory, from which the idea of molecules derived. Later in life, then, Hahnemann might have found out there probably were such things. But it's unlikely he could have realized the implications for his theory.

They've therefore proposed the idea that the active agent, even though completely absent because of the dilution, might have "imprinted" itself upon the water in such a way that its one-time presence is still felt. For this to be the case would require some revision of the known laws of physics. That, some homeopaths maintain, is the fault of physics, not the fault of homeopathy!

Other homeopaths propose that the supposed "memory" the water has of the active ingredient could be due to quantum entanglement.[1] Alas, although quantum entanglement is a genuine phenomenon, it's a flimsy one: Even under laboratory conditions it's extraordinary difficult to make an entanglement last longer than a tiny fraction of a second. There's no chance at all that entanglements could survive the multiple shakings involved in a homeopathic dilution. Besides, how would changing the state of a few subatomic particles turn water into a medicine?

There's a more fundamental problem with the "water's memory" claim. Any water we drink has had a long history—a history lasting billions of years. During that time it has been recycled in all sorts of ways, and has held all manner of other substances in solution, any one of which could have left an "imprint." Why should water retain the "memory" of a homeopathic molecule but not that of *everything else* with which it has been in contact—including all the gazillions of poops that have floated in it?

The notion of "water's memory" takes homeopathy over the conceptual border into the realm of outright woo—especially when we

---

1. The phenomenon operating at the quantum level whereby two particles that have interacted and then separated are still "linked" in that a change in a state of one (for example, its polarity) will instantaneously lead to the same change in the other.

read of some homeopaths claiming they can email the "imprint" to their patients, who can supply their own water! Even if you look just at basic homeopathy, though, of the kind that Hahnemann invented, the dilutions mean that all you get when you buy a homeopathic medicine is very expensive water.

On the plus side, it's pretty hard to do yourself any damage with a homeopathic overdose.

ACUPUNCTURE

In the same way that medieval physicians believed it was important for the healthy body to maintain a balance of the four humors, so did ancient Chinese physicians think the body should have a balance of the universal principles *yin* and *yang*. In terms of the body, these two principles can be thought of as, very roughly, chronic conditions (*yin*) and acute conditions (*yang*). Someone with a chronic condition like heart disease could thus be diagnosed as suffering an excess of *yin*; for someone who has a heart attack, the problem's too much *yang*. What keeps these principles in balance is the flow around the body of the life force, *qi* or *chi*, along a grid of pathways called meridians. Certain points on the meridians, nodes, relate to specific parts of the body. The function of the acupuncturist is to stick a needle into an appropriate node and, by manipulating it, affect the *chi* so as to re-establish the patient's *yin/yang* balance.

Today, little electric stimulators are often used in place of the needles. This reduces any discomfort the process might cause you (although traditional acupuncture is barely painful) and, more importantly, cuts the risk of infection. Alternatively, an ultrasound generator can be used. Yet another variant is acupressure, where the therapist just presses the relevant points rather than sticking needles into them.

The theory underpinning acupuncture is obviously nonsensical; for example, there's no such stuff as *chi*, and the meridians don't exist. But is it possible that acupuncture works *anyway*?

Normally, when testing a therapy—a new drug, perhaps—the method is to try it out on lots of volunteers. At the same time, lots of *other* volunteers either get no treatment or are given a placebo in place of the real drug. By analyzing what happens to the different groups of volunteers we can find out how effective the new drug is. This approach is far more difficult with acupuncture. You can't tell if the pill you're given contains a drug or just sugar, but you can certainly tell the difference between having needles stuck into you and *not* having needles stuck into you! One approach has been to apply the needles (or stimulators), but to the wrong places.

The results of trials done on acupuncture are confusing, even after the researchers have taken account of the placebo effect. What muddies the water is that results from some countries—China, Japan, Hong Kong, Taiwan, Russia—are overwhelmingly favorable while those from other countries are far less rosy, or even dismissive. No one's sure why—whether it's a matter of investigator bias (researchers who believe in acupuncture unconsciously skew their results to favor it) or subject bias (volunteers from cultures that traditionally favor acupuncture are more likely to report feeling better after a course of it).

One odd result is that it appears not to matter if the needles are applied to the nodes or not: any beneficial effect seems to come just from the sticking in of needles. In studies of the placebo effect it's been noticed that the *form* of the placebo influences the strength of the effect it has. No one knows for sure why this should be. The effect is strongest if injections are used. Might it be that the needles used in acupuncture likewise generate an abnormally strong placebo reaction? Again, we just don't know.

CANCER "CURES"

"Doctor" Ruth Drown made large sums of money through the 1930s and 1940s by claiming she could cure cancer and other diseases.

She did this using her Radio Therapeutic Instrument. This gadget was what is known to quack-hunters as a black box: a device with dials on the front, an electricity supply, perhaps flashing lights, cutesy little knobs to turn, and whatever else it might spring into the heart of the "inventor" to add to make the gadget look impressively technological even though it is in fact quite useless for anything except, well, looking impressively technological. Drown's black box, she said, was able to analyze patients' blood samples and thereby diagnose what was wrong.

It could also be used to cure people. Two wires came out of the box, with electrodes at their ends. Patients put one electrode on their feet and the other on their stomach to "complete the circuit." For the cure to work, the patient had to set the dials on the front of the machine to specific values, according to the diagnosis Drown had made.

This all sounds so hokey you'd think no one would be fooled by it. But in fact plenty of people paid big bucks to fraudsters like Drown. The type of quack medicine that involves a black box supposedly diagnosing illness from a sample of blood (or hair, or skin, or even handwriting) is known as radionics, and was first developed by a man called Albert Abrams.[1] Abrams made a fortune selling his black boxes. After a cancer patient who'd supposedly been completely cured died within weeks, in 1923, the American Medical Association (AMA) and the magazine *Scientific American* started investigations. Needless to say, they showed Abrams's radionics to be a complete sham. On one occasion a radionicist, using a blood sample, diagnosed a person as suffering from malaria, cancer, diabetes, and syphilis—which was really quite remarkable, because the blood had come from a chicken.

It was a cancer "cure" that brought about Ruth Drown's downfall, too. In 1948 a Mrs. Marguerite Rice of Illinois, frightened of having surgery to investigate a lump in her breast, instead chose to consult Drown, who referred her to one of her disciples. Sessions with the disciple were expensive, so Marguerite and her husband decided to buy their own Radio Therapeutic Instrument, and Marguerite spent several hours each day "completing the circuit." When that became tiresome, Drown told the Rices there was an alternative that was almost as good. Marguerite could put a sample of her blood on a piece of blotting paper and fasten that between the electrodes. The therapeutic influence of the gadget would continue to work even though Marguerite wasn't actually there beside it, and so she'd be able to treat herself for a full twenty-four hours each day, awake or asleep!

What's astonishing is that the Rices' Bullshitometer didn't go off long before Mr. Rice came across a newspaper article debunking Drown and her claims. At that point the Rices went to see a proper doctor,

---

1. Abrams also invented a medical treatment with the marvelous name of *spondylotherapy*. Rather like osteopathy and chiropractic, it involved manipulation around the spine.

and discovered that the cancer which might have been curable when Marguerite discovered the lump in her breast had by now metastasized (spread). The Rices contacted the AMA, which brought in the FDA.

At the trial, Drown's defense attorney called witnesses—including the mother of the actor Tyrone Power—who claimed to have had great results from Drown's therapy. Ask yourself why someone's evidence on a matter of medicine should be thought especially valuable simply because she's the mother of a famous actor. Apparently the jury thought so! Talk about a failure to evaluate your authorities . . .

Even so, Drown was found guilty.

Her punishment? A $1,000 fine. Moreover, she was allowed to continue to practice in her home state of California, just not to export her devices across the state lines. It took until 1963 for the California State Bureau to bring a case against her, and by the time that case could come to court, Drown had already died.

The saga of Ruth Drown pales beside that of Harry Hoxsey, who built a whole business empire on the basis of his claims to cure cancer. He began in the early 1920s and, because he bribed judges and senators, it was not until the late 1950s that the FDA was finally able to put him out of business; the death toll from his activities is incalculable.

He started off by treating external cancers using a method he claimed he'd been taught by his father.[1] This involved smearing a special paste on the affected area. Although Hoxsey didn't say so, the paste was years later found to contain arsenic. Arsenic has the property of killing nearby cells, including cancerous ones, so in a limited sense the "cure" worked—although obviously not if the cancer had metastasized.

---

1. His father had died in 1919. The cause of death? Cancer. Go figure.

Much later, Hoxsey and his employees treated internal cancers as well at their luxurious and expensive medical centers—and they had a high rate of success! This is because it was Hoxsey and his cronies who made the diagnoses. There is nothing easier to cure than the cancer of a patient who didn't have cancer in the first place.

People like Drown, Abrams, and Hoxsey were obvious frauds: they were in it for the money. But others have genuinely believed they've found ways to counter cancer, and not all have been obviously cranks. Linus Pauling won the Nobel Prize in Chemistry in 1954 and then the Nobel Peace Prize in 1962. Later in life he convinced himself cancer could be kept at bay using massive doses of vitamin C. Because of his distinguished career, people took him seriously, even after numerous experiments done by others had shown that the effects Pauling described were illusory.[1] He also advocated revolutionizing psychiatry by the introduction of what he called orthomolecular therapy, whereby vitamin supplements could be used to cure mental illness.

Many people have suggested that magnets—or an electromagnetic field—could defeat cancers. This notion really goes back to the ideas of the eighteenth-century quack Franz Anton Mesmer, who promoted the idea of a mysterious bodily energy flow that he called animal magnetism. (In the process he discovered what we today call the hypnotic state, but that's another story.) Through the nineteenth century, various perfectly sincere physicians—plus, of course, plenty of quacks—revealed the marvelous cures that magnets could effect.

---

1. Pauling may yet have the last laugh—at least in a limited way. Research by Yan Ma, Julia Chapman and others, published in the journal *Science Translational Medicine* in February 2014, showed that high doses of vitamin C, if injected rather than swallowed, as in earlier tests, inhibited ovarian cancer in mice and ameliorated the side-effects of chemotherapy in human ovarian-cancer patients.

REJECTING THE GERM THEORY

Today we know that infectious and contagious diseases are caused by microbes (germs)—viruses, bacteria, and fungi—but until the nineteenth century, infection was something of a mystery. Some physicians believed epidemics were caused by *miasmas*. Rotting corpses were a good candidate for these bad airs; after all, in times of plague there were always lots of rotting corpses about.

In the early nineteenth century, several physicians recognized that improving hygiene led to reductions in the spread of infection. For example, in the 1840s the obstetrician Ignaz Semmelweis managed to reduce the death rate of mothers from puerperal fever in the Vienna General Hospital's maternity wards from 18 percent to about 2 percent just by getting surgeons to wash their hands. The person who took the next step, producing what came to be known as the germ theory—that infection was spread by microscopic organisms—was the French scientist Louis Pasteur, working in the 1860s. In the 1870s, the UK surgeon Joseph Lister[1] pioneered the application of the germ theory to hospital practice, developing the forerunners of the kinds of sanitation we expect in hospitals today.

A rival of Pasteur, the French biologist Antoine Béchamp, claimed the basic building block of living organisms is not the cell but an entity he called the *microzyme*. Microzymes could take on different forms. Sick people's bodies were thus full of bacteria not because the malicious microbes had invaded from outside, but because some of the sufferers' microzymes were taking the form of bacteria. Béchamp's ideas are

---

1. One of whose students and disciples was my grandfather.

almost forgotten today.

Surprisingly, there are still a few people who, in the teeth of all the evidence, doubt the germ theory. Needless to say, these bullshitters aren't qualified mainstream physicians. One of the most prominent is the comedian Bill Maher. He attempts to justify his antivaxerism (see next chapter) by questioning the discovery that lies at the very heart of the enormous success of modern medical science: the germ theory.

Of all the US magnetic therapists of the nineteenth century, the most notorious must surely be C. J. Thacher, founder of the Chicago Magnetic Company and described by *Colliers Magazine* as the "king of the magnetic quacks." Thacher claimed not only that all sorts of cures could be effected by the application of magnets, but also that the wearing of magnets was the best way to assure one's health and well-being. To this end, his mail-order catalogue of 1866 advertised a huge range of magnetic garments; if you bought and wore a full set of these you'd be the proud owner of, reportedly, over seven hundred therapeutic magnets.[1] So insistent was Thacher about the therapeutic value of his magnets that it becomes almost tempting to believe he was genuine. But some of the stories he told of the cures he achieved—such as having paralysis victims up and walking within moments—make it plain he was a liar and quack.

---

1. Luckily it'd be a few decades yet before you'd have to worry about what'd happen when you put these garments into an electric washing machine.

Sadly, after a period in the doldrums, notions concerning the supposed therapeutic influence of magnets have come back into prominence in the guise of what is called *magnetic therapy*, *magnetic field therapy*, or *magnetotherapy*. One reason for the resurgence in the belief that magnets affect health was that, from the 1970s, some researches began to suggest there might be a link between strong electromagnetic fields and cancer. This culminated in the early 1990s with various legal cases claiming that sufferers had developed cancers because of electromagnetic fields associated with the power lines or transformers near their homes. The lawyers for the plaintiffs were able to point at a scientific literature that offered some guarded support. Guarded or otherwise, the support soon withered and the cases were kicked out.

A US estimate early in the twenty-first century indicated that annual national sales of therapeutic magnets were anywhere between $200 and $500 million. Go online and within minutes you will find countless traders willing to sell you therapeutic magnets, although usually they're careful to indicate in the small print that no actual therapeutic result is guaranteed. Reliance on such trinkets is apparently now endemic among sportsmen and -women, who wear them much as one might carry a lucky shamrock. Golfers, meanwhile, can buy expensive magnetic shoes, which supposedly improve circulation and thereby prevent fatigue; as Christopher Wanjek comments in his book *Bad Medicine* (2003), they must also cause some worried moments if a thunderstorm starts.

Göesta Wollin, coauthor with Erick Endby of the book *Curing Cancer with Supermagnets* (1987), made a business out of marketing so-called Neomax magnets—the "supermagnets" of the title—which were made out of iron, boron, and neodymium. Wollin recommended that his magnets be worn around the neck like a locket, and claimed success treating breast cancer. He added that "this type of treatment does not damage healthy cells because healthy cells have different electromagnetic potential than cancer cells." They do?

James D. Livingston, who eviscerated the claims of Wollin and others in his entertaining book *Driving Force: The Natural Magic of Magnets* (1996), tried to clarify matters:

> The miraculous effects of supermagnets are explained by the authors' "universal spiral theory," which is based on the observation that spirals are found throughout nature, from galaxies down to DNA. They propose that because the spirals in the supermagnets are bigger than the spirals in the cancer cells, the magnets eventually kill the cancer . . .

Oh, the power of spiral bullshit.

The web is full of other "cures" for cancer, as you'll discover if you spend a few minutes tooling around with a search engine; the Laetrile case is discussed briefly at the start of the next chapter. For some reason, bogus cancer cures also seem popular among the far-right websites and ezines, which frequently push them either as self-promoting articles by unorthodox physicians or as paid advertising from those same unorthodox physicians (it's often hard to tell the difference). A frequently recurring theme is that, even though dozens of adoring testimonials from his patients show Dr. Bonkers has discovered a dynamic cure for cancer, the AMA and/or the FDA (or even FEMA!) is striving to shut him down; apparently the medical establishment is resistant to the discovery of a cancer cure. So the account feeds into the conspiracy-theory/coverup obsessions of the readers.

In reality, of course, anyone who *did* find a cancer cure would be instantly famous, would be celebrated to the skies by the medical establishment, and would enjoy untold riches and eventually a Nobel Prize, just among the more obvious rewards.

🚫

4. IMPLACABLE FOES OF REASON: THE ANTIVAXERS

Dan Burton, a US Congressman from 1983 until retiring in 2013, has a habit of thinking he knows more about medicine than medical professionals do.

In 1977, for example, he believed he knew more than the FDA did about Laetrile, a chemical that was supposed to be effective in curing cancer. The FDA, which has a "controversial" habit of investigating purported cancer cures, said that not only did Laetrile not work but that patients who used the stuff ran the risk of cyanide poisoning.[1] Even so, Burton fought hard to have the use of Laetrile legalized in his home state of Indiana. According to a 1999 report:

> "I think every opportunity should be given to people," [Burton] stated, "so that they can survive and have a healthy life, and many times, hope alone and belief that they are going to get better is one of the ingredients that makes them get better."

Yes, optimism can be a good thing when you're sick. Cyanide? Not so much.

Dan Burton has always been a great supporter of the supplements

---

1. Enzymes in the body can react with Laetrile to produce cyanide compounds.

industry. He's one of the reasons why the US, unlike the rest of the developed world, has no proper regulation of the contents of those cute little bottles of vitamins and minerals that tempt you from the supermarket shelves. Congress has hugely limited the powers of the FDA to do *anything* to control the supplements manufacturers: you have no guarantee that the pills or capsules contain what the label says they do, there's no proper hygiene oversight of their manufacture, et cetera. The one thing the FDA *can* do is take action after the contents of the bottle have been discovered to be actually poisonous.

It did this in 1997 when new scientific research raised the alarm about a substance called ephedra. Ephedra, derived from certain species of thistle, has been used in Chinese and other traditional medicines. The new research showed that even small quantities of ephedra had caused cases of cardiac arrest, horrendous mental problems, and even death. The FDA therefore tried to ban it from use in supplements.

Dan Burton again thought he knew better. Thanks to his efforts, it took until 2004 before the FDA could get this potentially lethal substance removed from sale.

DR. WAKEFIELD'S CONTROVERSY

So it's hardly surprising that Dan Burton took UK physician Dr. Andrew Wakefield to his heart when Wakefield, the darling of the antivaxers,[1] came to the US.

---

1. Some people use the spelling "anti-vaxxers." I prefer the form used here. How *do* you pronounce a double "x"?

Almost since the principle of vaccination was discovered by Edward Jenner[1] in the late eighteenth century, people have been looking for reasons to be frightened of it. Jenner's breakthrough was to infect people with the relatively mild disease cowpox and thereby give them immunity to the extremely dangerous disease smallpox. Thanks to the vaccination, smallpox rates fell, and then, in the twentieth century, plummeted; the disease was finally eliminated in 1977.

Even from early on, although vaccination against smallpox obviously had the power to save millions of human lives, many otherwise intelligent people campaigned against it. One of them was the playwright George Bernard Shaw; his antivaxer vehemence was all the more astonishing because the disease had nearly killed him in childhood.

Andrew Wakefield first hit the medical headlines in 1995. He and his colleagues at the Royal Free Hospital in London had been working on Crohn's disease, a disease of the gastrointestinal tract with complications that can be extremely serious; no one's yet sure what causes it. When the team published a paper in the major medical journal *Lancet* called "Is Measles Vaccination a Risk Factor for Inflammatory Bowel Disease?" there was a minor sensation.

They proposed that Crohn's disease was caused by the measles virus hanging around in the body long after the actual measles has passed. Though wrong, this wasn't a totally outlandish idea. (For example, the chickenpox virus remains in the body after the chickenpox has gone, and years or decades later can cause the quite different disease called shingles.) What raised the furor was that the team claimed the measles

---

1. Jenner may not have been the first, but he's usually given the credit.

vaccine[1] could give the same result—i.e., that being vaccinated against measles could lead to getting Crohn's disease.

Scientists worldwide worked to replicate the team's results, but couldn't. In August 1998 the team published another paper, this time in the *Journal of Medical Virology*, which basically admitted they'd gotten it wrong.

By then, however, Wakefield had a new and improved hypothesis: the MMR vaccine could cause autism. The idea was that the vaccine did physical damage to the intestine that released toxic proteins into the bloodstream; when those proteins reached the brain, they made the person autistic.

He and his colleagues outlined this hypothesis in another *Lancet* paper, but before it was published, Wakefield called a press conference to tell the world about his deductions. Since Wakefield is a very persuasive speaker, what should have been regarded as at most a tentative hypothesis was taken by the journalists to be cutting-edge science. The UK news media went into full-scale panic mode . . . and stayed that way long after medical science had determined that the conclusion was false.

One of Wakefield's senior co-authors,[2] Simon Murch, perhaps said it best:

---

1. Usually delivered as the MMR, measles-mumps-rubella, vaccine.
2. The word "co-author" has a somewhat different meaning for scientific publications than it does ordinarily. Often you'll find a dozen or even a hundred people listed as co-authors of a scientific paper. This doesn't mean they all did a share of the writing. Probably no more than one or two people actually wrote the paper. The rest contributed research or, sometimes, didn't even do that. There's a lot of debate in the scientific world about "co-authors" who've merely lent their names to papers.

RUNNING WITH THE HERD

An important concept when talking about vaccination is *herd immunity*. A few infants have hereditary conditions that make it a bad idea for them to be vaccinated. In some other infants, while vaccination isn't dangerous, for various reasons it's ineffective.

The fact that a small number of people in a community aren't immune to measles doesn't matter much. So long as everybody else is, the disease can't get a foothold and the community as a whole is safe. The problem comes when levels of immunization fall too far for the "herd" to be immune. And that's exactly what has happened in many countries that had thought they'd freed themselves from the scourge of measles and whooping cough, including many parts of the US.

This link [between MMR vaccination and autism] is unproven and measles is a killing infection. If this precipitates a scare and immunization rates go down, as sure as night follows day, measles will return and children will die.

Murch was proved exactly right. Measles had been virtually eradicated from the UK and Ireland but, after the media scare campaign, many parents were reluctant to have their children vaccinated with MMR. Whole communities lost their herd immunity (see sidebar). Now, measles has become an endemic disease in England and Wales; there have been several deaths. An outbreak in Dublin in 1999–2000

THE BODY COUNT

If you want a sobering experience, look at the website Anti-Vaccine Body Count.[1] The site keeps a running total of the number of vaccine-preventable illnesses and deaths in the US since June 3, 2007. (2007 was the year a number of celebrity antivaxers began to make a noise.) As the website says, "The Anti-Vaccination Movement has a body count attached to its name."

When I last checked, in November 2014, the figures had last been updated on September 6: The number of preventable illnesses stood at 139,199 and the number of preventable deaths at 6,265. The number of autism diagnoses scientifically linked to vaccinations stood, as it always has, at 0.

---

1. http://www.antivaccinebodycount.com.

hospitalized over a hundred children, of whom a dozen required intensive care and three died. Other countries have had similar experiences. As well as deaths, there have been instances of people being afflicted so badly they'll be disabled for the rest of their lives.

In the US it's been a bit different. The disease was essentially eliminated from the country by the early 2000s. However, thanks to the efforts of US antivaxers, there have been several outbreaks since then. Unvaccinated people who go abroad to countries where measles is prevalent can bring the disease back with them. And they can infect unvaccinated people in the US—or even people who *have* been vaccinated but the vaccination hasn't taken.

And it's not just measles. In late 2010, because of falling vaccination rates against whooping cough (pertussis), California suffered its worst outbreak of that disease in over half a century: thousands were infected, and at least ten babies died.

It's not all bad news, however. Although antivaxer campaigns in some countries have increased the measles rates in those regions, globally the picture is improving. In early 2014, the World Health Organization revealed that, between 2000 and 2012, annual deaths worldwide from measles went down from over 562,000 to about 122,000. That's about a 78 percent drop. Reported cases of measles dropped by almost exactly the same percentage. There's no room for complacency—measles is still a killer disease and the death toll is still horrific—but progress is being made.

And it's coming about almost entirely because of vaccination.

INCOMPETENCE OR FRAUD?

A journalist called Brian Deer was suspicious of Wakefield's claims from the outset, and for years he researched the background of that notorious 1998 *Lancet* paper.

He unearthed that Wakefield had been paid chunky sums of money by a lawyer called Robert Barr, who was involved in a class-action lawsuit against the manufacturers of the MMR vaccine. It just happened that the conclusions of the *Lancet* paper were very useful to Barr's case. Of the twelve children who were the subjects of Wakefield's work, several were the children of Barr's clients. The antivaxer group JABS (for Justice Awareness and Basic Support) was also involved with Wakefield, and had supplied some of the other children. There were errors in the way the experiments were done and the results recorded.

Worst of all, the team had committed ethical breaches. For example, they had subjected eight of the children to colonoscopies even though there was no good medical reason to do this. A colonoscopy involves (to simplify) sticking a camera up your rear end, and the sensation is highly unpleasant. It can be risky, too—in fact, one of the unfortunate kids suffered accidental damage to the colon. Techniques like colonoscopies are called "invasive procedures" (you bet they are!), and there are strict rules about their use in research. The subjects here were autistic children. Inflicting colonoscopies and other invasive procedures on them was nothing short of abuse.

By 2004, Deer had found so many reasons to doubt the veracity of Wakefield's paper that ten of Wakefield's co-authors on it had withdrawn their names.* The General Medical Council (GMC), which regulates the medical profession in the UK, set up an inquiry. Years later, in 2010, the investigation reported a whole string of dishonesties and abuses associated with the paper and the GMC decided that Andrew Wakefield and one of his co-authors, John Walker-Smith, should lose their licenses to practice as doctors. In 2011, the *British Medical Journal* published three articles by Brian Deer arguing that Wakefield's work wasn't just flawed and dishonest, but actually fraudulent.

THIOMERSAL—THE WRONG SUSPECT

By the time Deer's article was published and Wakefield lost his license to practice medicine, he was already living in the US, having left his homeland early in the 2000s. He was greeted as something of a hero by the antivaxer community in this country, which included several important politicians: John Kerry, Chris Dodd, Joe Lieberman, and our old friend Congressman Dan Burton, who in 1997 had become Chairman of the House Government Reform Committee, a position of considerable power.

Burton's grandson Christian began showing symptoms of autism in infancy. Looking around for something to blame, the distraught grandfather connected this to the batch of vaccinations the child had received a few weeks earlier.

In particular, Burton focused on a substance called thiomersal (or thimerosal—both versions are correct), an antiseptic of which tiny quantities were added to vaccines as a preservative.[1] thiomersal is a compound of mercury, and mercury is known to cause brain damage. The connection was obvious.

Well, not really.

Whenever you talk about whether or not something's poisonous, one important factor is the dosage. Although we've all read detective stories in which the murderer used arsenic to kill the victim, your body *needs* very small quantities of arsenic in its diet if it's to function properly. (There have even been cases of arsenic addiction.) On the other side of the coin, everyone knows that water is vital to life . . . but if you drink too much of it you can actually kill yourself. In both cases, what's important is the dose. The amount of thiomersal used in vaccines was so tiny that it was hard to understand how it might do any harm.

---

1. Before people started adding preservatives, vaccines could become dangerously infected by other bugs.

Another point worth remembering is that mercury poisoning produces very specific symptoms. No one's ever reported thiomersal producing those symptoms.

One more thing. Thiomersal is a mercury *compound*. Compounds usually behave very differently than do the elements of which they're made. For example, you wouldn't want to swallow sodium, because it bursts into flames when put in water, and chlorine was used in World War I as a weapon—it's a poisonous gas. But if you put the two together you get sodium chloride: table salt. Similarly, the mercury in thiomersal is tied up with other elements. When the thiomersal hits the bloodstream it breaks down, with one of the products—the mercury-containing one—being ethylmercury. This flushes from the body within about two and a half weeks.

Of course, it's all very well to say that thiomersal *shouldn't* cause any harm. That doesn't mean that in practice it *can't*.

Several huge sets of clinical trials have shown no adverse effects of the use of thiomersal in vaccines. But you could argue that a link between thiomersal and autism might not be easy to spot.

Except that we have the best test of all. From the late 1990s, because of the activities of the antivaxers, the vaccine manufacturers found substitute preservatives in place of thiomersal. They didn't do this because they thought thiomersal was dangerous. It was just that, with memories of legal farragoes like the silicone-breast-implant panic fresh in mind (see page 140), they didn't want to find themselves at the wrong end of multi-billion-dollar class-action lawsuits with outcomes decided on the basis of pseudoscience.

If Burton and the other antivaxers had been correct about the dangers of thiomersal, we'd surely have seen a decline in the rates of autism now that the substance wasn't being used. In fact, the autism rates continued to rise.

This is all the more remarkable because, as we saw, vaccination rates have fallen calamitously because of the panic.

Let's get this straight. *Fewer* children are being vaccinated but *more* children are contracting autism. If the antivaxers were right, the autism figures should be dropping along with the vaccination rates, shouldn't they?

Unless, of course, the antivaxers are wrong.

That's the simplest explanation of all these contradictions, isn't it?

A NEVERENDING STORY

Wakefield's 1998 *Lancet* paper didn't suggest that thiomersal played any role in autism; it fingered the dead measles virus as the culprit. This didn't stop Dan Burton from welcoming Andrew Wakefield as a kindred soul. In 2000, Burton, as Chairman of the House Government Reform Committee, held a hearing on the relationship between the MMR vaccine and autism. He called for testimony from a parade of the very few scientists he could find to support his belief, and Andrew Wakefield was his star turn.

Congress was wise enough to recognize this performance as just a piece of theater, and declined to ban vaccination, which was what Burton wanted. However, the "news" media and the public went wild. The flames were fanned again a few years later, in June 2005, when Robert F. Kennedy Jr.'s article "Deadly Immunity" appeared in *Rolling Stone*. Kennedy accused thiomersal again.

People began to believe that the way to cure autism was to get the infant's body to expel all the mercury left over from the vaccination. Soon there was a new term on everybody's lips: chelation therapy.

Poisoning by heavy metals like mercury, iron, arsenic, and lead is no joke. One way to reduce the quantities of these elements in the body is to introduce substances that combine with them to produce harmless compounds that then easily flush out. Used professionally, chelation therapy can be very helpful in cases of acute metal poisoning.

Some of the parents whose children suffer from autism, believing the problem is some kind of mercury poisoning because of the thiomersal, have tried chelation therapy to reduce the (supposed) mercury levels.

As we saw, mercury poisoning isn't the problem in cases of autism—especially since thiomersal is rarely used in vaccines now!—and any self-styled "chelation therapists" who sell their services to parents as an autism cure are effectively taking money for nothing. The same goes for the marketing of chelation therapy to cancer and cardiovascular patients: you'd be just as well off clutching your lucky shamrock. The American Cancer Society (ACS) states bluntly:

> According to a number of well-respected organizations, including the American Heart Association, the American Medical Association, the Centers for Disease Control and Prevention, the American Osteopathic Association, the American Academy of Family Physicians, and the FDA, there is no scientific evidence that chelation therapy is an effective treatment for any medical condition except heavy metal poisoning.

In fact, you might be *better off* with that shamrock, because the ACS adds:

> Chelation therapy may produce toxic effects, including kidney damage, irregular heart beat, and swelling of the veins. It may also cause nausea, vomiting, diarrhea, and temporary lowering of blood pressure. Since the therapy removes minerals from the body, there is a risk of developing low calcium levels (hypocalcemia) and bone damage. Chelation therapy may also impair the immune system and decrease the body's ability to produce insulin. People may also feel pain at the site of the EDTA injection. Chelation therapy may be dangerous in people with kidney disease, liver disease, or bleeding disorders. Women who are pregnant or breastfeeding should not use this method.

Two of the physicians offering chelation therapy as a treatment for autism, the father-and-son colleagues Mark and David Geier, also theorized that, since far more boys than girls suffer from autism, the problem might relate to the unlucky boys having too much testosterone. So the Geiers began using a chemical-castration treatment alongside the chelation therapy . . . Luckily, before this went too far, the scientific community had demolished most of the Geiers' claims.

With huge trials having shown zero connection between vaccination and autism—such as the one run in Denmark in 1991-98 that studied over half a million children—and with overwhelming evidence having emerged that autism is a genetically based condition, it might seem that it was long past time for the antivaxers to shut up shop. No such luck.

Although many antivaxers have recognized that the absence of thiomersal from vaccines means its mercury can no longer be blamed for autism, some have shifted their attention to formaldehyde. While formaldehyde isn't good for you if you have too much of it, our bodies need small amounts to function properly. It's used during the preparation of vaccines and, even though it's removed before the vaccine is delivered, there are tiny amounts still left. These are far lower than the levels the Environmental Protection Agency (EPA) considers safe—far lower, too, than the amount you'd take in if you ate an apple! Since we don't see antivaxers warning you about the gross dangers of eating apples . . .

If formaldehyde won't fit the bill, what about antifreeze? A number of antivaxers have kicked up a furor over the fact that vaccines contain polyethylene glycol. Antifreeze uses ethylene glycol, which is toxic. Surely those two substances are the same? Well, no, they aren't. They're different substances with different properties, as you'd expect from the fact that one has a "poly" in its name and the other doesn't. The most important difference in this context is that, while ethylene glycol is toxic, polyethylene glycol isn't.

SO WHY HAVE THE AUTISM RATES CONTINUED TO RISE?

Since the causes of autism are so very poorly understood, no one's really sure why the rates continue to rise. (Similarly not well understood is why about four times as many boys as girls are affected.)

One factor might be that fewer cases are going unreported. In the

CHICKENPOX PARTIES

Perhaps the most horrifying antic of this country's antivaxers is the so-called Chickenpox Party. Chickenpox isn't as dangerous a disease as measles, although it too can kill; it's more dangerous if contracted in adulthood. The idea of a Chickenpox Party is to immunize a whole bunch of kids by gathering them together with an infected child. That way the children can catch the disease and, after some suffering, be immune to it for the rest of their lives (although vulnerable to shingles later on—see page 163). Of course, the children would be significantly safer if they were vaccinated instead, but try telling this to a fanatic.

The same approach has been taken by some misguided parents to other diseases, including measles, mumps, and hepatitis A. These are seriously life-threatening illnesses, so grouping uninfected children with an infected child is really a murderous activity. Even worse, campaigns have been mounted on the internet persuading gullible parents to send each other infected items—typically lollipops—so that kids can infect each other by mail. This is actually against the law but, more importantly, while the chickenpox virus is unlikely to survive long enough on the lollipop to infect the recipient, *other* viruses that the donor child might have—some of them deadly—could very well do so.

past, many parents and even doctors probably thought children whom we'd now say were autistic were merely mentally retarded. As more and more physicians and others have become aware of the disease, it's likely to be diagnosed earlier and more frequently.

Another factor is that several neurodevelopmental conditions once thought to be distinct from autism are now recognized as being related to it. These include Asperger Syndrome and Rett Syndrome. Doctors now talk about an *autism spectrum* rather than about a single disease. So part of the apparent increase in rates of autism may be that some kids are being included in the tally today where previously they wouldn't have been.

In a scientific paper published in March 2014, Philippe Grandjean and Philip J. Landrigan pointed the finger at environmental pollution by various industrial chemicals that are known to be developmental neurotoxicants—i.e., to damage the brains of developing infants. Among the conditions they include is autism. According to the Harvard School of Public Health press release about the paper, Grandjean and Landrigan forecast that many more chemicals than the known dozen or so identified as neurotoxicants contribute to a "silent pandemic" of neurobehavioral deficits that is eroding intelligence, disrupting behaviors, and damaging societies. But controlling this pandemic is difficult because of a scarcity of data to guide prevention and the huge amount of proof needed for government regulation. "Very few chemicals have been regulated as a result of developmental neurotoxicity," they write.

Susanne Atanus, a 2014 nominee for Illinois's 9th Congressional District, has a rather more radical explanation for autism. According to the local newspaper, the *Daily Herald*, in January 2014 she said "she believes God controls the weather and has put tornadoes and diseases such as autism and dementia on earth in response to gay rights and legalized abortions."

OTHER VACCINES

Some antivaxers have moved on to mount scare campaigns about other vaccines. A frequent claim is that the incurable disease polio is spread by the polio vaccine. Since the disease was initially identified in the first half of the nineteenth century and polio vaccines didn't come along until the middle of the twentieth, after which polio rates plummeted, this might seem a difficult case to make.

According to one version of this conjecture, polio was just about to die out anyway when the appearance of the vaccines revived it. The figures tell a different story. In the developed world, polio rates did indeed gently decline from the late nineteenth century onward, primarily because of improving hygiene. But they remained obscenely high by today's standards. The first polio vaccine to come into widespread use was developed by Jonas Salk and licensed in the US in 1955. Official figures show that, between 1954 and 1961, the annual US polio rate dropped about 96.5 percent, from 38,476 cases to just 1,312. By 1994 the disease had disappeared from the Americas. That doesn't really indicate a big revival caused by the vaccine!

Another favorite antivaxer target is the annual flu vaccine. Frequently there'll be reference to the fact that the US swine flu vaccination program in 1976 killed more people than the flu itself did. This sounds pretty grim until you think about it: the more effective the vaccine, the fewer deaths from the flu! But there's another sense in which it's misleading.

The 1976 swine flu outbreak started in February of that year: it killed one soldier and hospitalized four others at Fort Dix, New Jersey. The medical authorities discovered that the strain of flu involved was very like the one that had killed millions worldwide in 1918, so they advised a mass vaccination. Because of political and other wrangles, the vaccination didn't start until October—months after the flu had defied all predictions by failing to spread further than Fort Dix. Three elderly people died soon after being vaccinated; although there was never any medical reason to believe the deaths were related to the vaccine, the media had a field day.

There were also claims that some people contracted the nasty neuro-muscular disorder Guillain-Barré syndrome (GBS) through being vaccinated. Later studies showed that it's possible there was a very slight increase in rates of GBS onset—about one case per 100,000 vaccinations. Studies of the vaccines used in other years almost invariably show no such increase; in a couple of instances, there might have been an increase of perhaps one case for every *million* vaccinations.

Overall, then, the 1976 situation was a very unusual one. The outbreak was, unexpectedly, very brief and confined to a very small area. Also, the vaccination campaign was botched. All told, at the very most, about twenty-five people died because of the vaccine; it's quite possible the figure was much lower, and feasible that no one did. That was in consequence of 48,161,019 people being vaccinated. To get the figure in proportion, about fifty people die each year in the US—twice as many—through being struck by lightning.

And what if the 1976 swine flu had indeed spread as it could have done? We might have expected at least as many deaths as in the average flu season. That number, for the US, is *about 30,000*.

Think about that number the next time someone tells you flu shots are dangerous.

MARTYRS

In some parts of the world, people are resisting polio vaccination for religious and/or conspiracy-theory reasons. As a result, the disease is still endemic in Nigeria, Afghanistan, and Pakistan. In the first two countries, progress in being made in eradicating it—although there was a temporary setback in 2003 in Nigeria when the governor of Kano state, believing vaccination was a western plot to sterilize Muslim women and spread AIDS, banned the procedure. Ten months later, when the disease had spread to neighboring states, he was persuaded to change his tune and a crash vaccination program started.

In Pakistan, though, resistance from the Taliban and other extremist Muslim groups is causing a real problem, and the infection rates are horrifying. So are the terrorist activities of these militant antivaxers. In a single week in January 2014, for example, three health workers were murdered in Karachi and, the next day, a bomb in the Charsadda district killed six cops who were guarding polio workers, injured nine others, and also killed a child. These are not isolated incidents.

A POTENTIALLY DEADLY DOSE FOR GIRLS?

If I asked you to name some supposedly fact-based TV shows or channels that habitually purvey purest bullshit, I'm sure you could reel off half a dozen before I'd even finished the question. There's *that* much bullshit on TV.

A NEUROTOXIN BY ANY OTHER NAME . . .

Jenny McCarthy, maybe the world's highest-profile antivaxer, has frequently argued that vaccines must obviously be dangerous because thiomersal contains mercury and mercury is a neurotoxin. As we've already noticed, this is to ignore two facts:

- Thiomersal isn't used in vaccines any more.
- Some things that are poisonous in larger doses are harmless or even beneficial in tiny ones.

A good example of the latter is the botulinum toxin, among the most deadly neurotoxins known. In *tiny* doses, however, it has useful medical properties—as McCarthy should know. "I love Botox, I absolutely love it," she declared in 2009. "I get it minimally, so I can still move my face. But I really do think it's a savior."

And the active principle in Botox is . . . ?

But sometimes the bullshit-mongers can be harder to spot, especially when the purveyor is otherwise a respected journalist. Here's an example from December 2013. The respected broadcaster was Katie Couric, the show was the ABC daytime talk show *Katie*, and the press materials issued before the airing read in part:

> The HPV vaccine is considered a life-saving cancer preventer . . . but is it a potentially deadly dose for girls?

Meet a mom who claims her daughter died after getting the HPV vaccine, and hear all sides of the HPV vaccine controversy.

In the broadcast, Couric interviewed

- the mother of a girl who died a couple of weeks after receiving the vaccine,
- a young woman who suffered multiple unexplained symptoms not long after receiving the vaccine, and
- Dr. Diane Harper, one of the rare qualified physicians who has given support to the antivaxers.

Set against this array was a single physician to express the consensus view of qualified doctors and medical scientists all over the world that the HPV vaccine is overwhelmingly safe. In other words, viewers were asked to compare the reasoned, dispassionate voice of science with the emotional personal testimonies. No wonder that many people came away from the show believing there was a raging controversy over the vaccine's safety.

Yet, if you look at the first two testimonies above, you can see that neither is very persuasive. Both, in fact, fall into the trap of confusing correlation with causation. People get ill and even die all the time; inevitably this sometimes happens not long after they've been vaccinated. It also sometimes happens not long after they've watched the Super Bowl!

HPV, or human papillomavirus, is very nasty indeed. Every year, in the US alone, it causes thousands of cases of cervical cancer, throat cancer, and anal cancer. These are particularly life-threatening cancers.

Anything that can be done to help prevent them is surely a good thing.

So, what's this controversy about the HPV vaccine that Couric and her producers talked about?

So far as medical science is concerned, there isn't a controversy. In a paper published in 2013 in the *British Medical Journal*, Scandinavian researchers reported on a study they'd done between October 2006 and December 2010 of 997,000 teenaged girls. Of these, 296,000 had been given at least one dose of the HPV vaccine.

In this massive study—nearly a million subjects!—the researchers could find no indication that the HPV vaccine caused any health problems whatsoever, in either the short or the long term.

In the US, the CDC tracked, between 2006 and 2009, the recipients of over 600,000 doses of the HPV vaccine. Again they could find no health risk from the vaccine.

Other studies have come to the same conclusion. The "controversy" that Katie Couric talked about in her TV show was a complete invention—bullshit deployed in hopes of attracting gullible viewers and consequent advertising revenue, no matter the number of people who might die because frightened off the vaccination.

🚫

5. NO HOAX: THE TRUTH ABOUT CLIMATE CHANGE

Ask yourself a simple question: If 98 percent of aeronautical engineers said a plane wasn't flightworthy, would you fly in that plane?

Here's another: If you needed brain surgery, would you get your plumber to do it?

I assume you'd answer "no" to both questions. Only a lunatic would ignore the warnings of the aeronautical engineers and fly in the plane. And only a lunatic would think a plumber the best choice to perform brain surgery.

Yet the huge army of people who're trying to persuade us that climate change is nothing to worry about are telling us we should ignore the warnings of 98 percent of the world's climate scientists.

And they're telling us that media bloviators and dentists can do just as good a job of climate science as climate scientists can.

What kind of lunatics do they think we are?

POLAR VORTEX BLUES

Early in 2014, much of the central and eastern part of North America was subjected to an extended period of freezing temperatures and repeated heavy snowfall. Cue the radio and TV bloviators, who started rehashing all their tired old falsehoods about how the world's not really

CLIMATEGATE

The term "Climategate" was coined by denialists after a large batch of private emails and other files was hacked from the backup server of the Climate Research Unit (CRU) at the University of East Anglia, UK. The material was put online, and then was promptly cherry picked by denialist outfits such as TV weatherman Anthony Watts's website *Watts Up With That?*

The cherry pickers and quote miners did their best to give the impression of a cadre of villainous climate scientists who were misleading the public into thinking there was a crisis. Unfortunately for the denialists' efforts, there wasn't much to work with. Certainly there were

warming but cooling.

At the very same time, California was suffering a massive drought, the UK was experiencing the worst flooding in living memory, the Australian summer was marked by record-breaking temperatures (some of the scheduling of the Australian Open tennis tournament had to be revised because it was simply too hot on the courts for the players' safety), and the organizers of the Winter Olympics at Sochi, Russia, were having to import snow; climatologists were predicting that, by the time of the 2022 Winter Olympics, none of the five current applicants to host it might in fact, because of rising temperatures, be able to do so.

So much for global cooling.

Why, then, *was* part of North America experiencing such bitter cold?

examples of scientists being rude about others, especially about climate-change denialists. The cherry pickers went into overdrive about a reference the CRU's head, Dr. Phil Jones, had made to a mathematical "trick" he'd discovered for manipulating a certain set of data; surely the word "trick" implied dishonesty? Well, no: He was talking merely about a mathematical technique.

There have been eight separate investigations of the activities at the CRU, and the climate scientists have been given a clean bill of health: There was no scientific misconduct, no deception. This hasn't stopped the denialists from referring to Climategate as if it were proof of their conspiracy theory.

A few decades ago, when it became clear that the warming of the planet was a serious problem, climate scientists might have been wiser to use the term "global weirding" rather than "global warming" to describe what was going on. This isn't to say that the atmosphere (or at least the part of it we live in, the troposphere) *isn't* warming: It most certainly is. But "global weirding" might have been an easier description for the public to accept when confronted by bizarre bits of weather that aren't always warm.

If you lived in central or eastern North America during the early part of 2014, you'll have encountered the term "polar vortex" before. As has been known since the middle of the nineteenth century, our planet has two polar vortexes, one at the north and the other at the south; the Arctic vortex has centers over Siberia and northern Canada's

Baffin Island. Essentially, the polar vortexes are permanent hurricanes,[1] stronger in winter than in summer. Because the Arctic is warming, the polar vortex has become weaker in recent years.

This has affected the polar jet stream, a persistent strong wind at the top of the troposphere. The weaker the polar vortex, the more the jet stream meanders in its course as it goes from west to east around the pole. This allows cold air from the Arctic—which, although it is warming,[2] is still a lot colder than most of us are used to—to penetrate much farther south than usual. And the jet stream, being weakened, tends to go round those regions of cold air rather than help dissipate them, so they hang about longer.

That North American cold in early 2014 was, then, directly attributable to global warming, even though the people shivering through it might have found it hard to understand that they were experiencing a dose of cold *weather* in the middle of a *climate* that was, overall, getting warmer.

A lot of people get weather and climate confused, so it's worth spending a moment making sure we know what the two words mean.

Weather is short-term and local. It might have *seemed* as if the cold spell of early 2014 lasted forever if you were in the middle of it, but in reality it was just a few weeks. Furthermore, it affected only a relatively small part of the globe: elsewhere people were experiencing very different weather.

Climate, on the other hand, is a long-term phenomenon. Usually when we talk about climate, we're thinking of a much larger

---

1. I'm using the term "hurricanes" in a generic way. Everything said here applies to typhoons and cyclones.
2. So is the Antarctic, of course, but it's the Arctic that's relevant here.

region than just a chunk of North America; most usually today, because of concerns about global warming, the "region" concerned is the whole world.

Here's an analogy that might help. A good day for the traders on Wall Street doesn't mean that *every* share price goes up: just that most of them do, and so the average does. Behind that rising average are plenty of share prices staying much the same and some that are dropping precipitously. Likewise with global temperatures: The average is rising calamitously, but there are local, short-term variations.

We can't point to a single extreme weather event—a hurricane, a drought, a catastrophic rainfall—and say it was caused by global warming. But every extreme weather event we see today has a bit of climate change in it. For example, when Hurricane Sandy pounded the northeastern seaboard in 2012, it would have been wrong to say that Sandy was caused by climate change. On the other hand, the reason that Sandy was where it was had to do with the weakening of the polar vortex—which, as we've seen, was a consequence of the warming Arctic. When the hurricane hit, New York State, which had planned in accordance with climate science, was proportionately less damaged than New Jersey, whose governor had rejected such planning.

The amount of snowfall in early 2014 was a result of there being more water in the atmosphere. Again, this is a consequence of overall warming—see below.

Because of climate change we can expect more hurricanes in the future, we can expect them to be more violent, and we can expect them more often to reach places where hurricanes didn't use to.

Why?

THE HOLES WHERE THE CO_2 LEAKS OUT

In the 1970s and 1980s, scientists became concerned that the ozone layer—the layer in the upper atmosphere that shields us from the sun's harmful ultraviolet radiation—was being damaged because of manufactured chemicals called CFCs that were in those days widely used in fridges, et cetera. The countries of the world for once took united action and, since the introduction of the Montreal Protocol in 1987, the use of CFCs has been phased out.

(Just to depress you, in early 2014 scientists at the University of East Anglia reported that the ozone layer was under threat again from four new manmade gases not covered by the Montreal Protocol. The hunt's now on to find out who's manufacturing these gases so they can be persuaded to stop before Australian cancer rates start rocketing.)

What has this to do with global warming? Not much, in terms of the science. But a 2006 Canadian study found many of the

Often when you read articles about climate change there's a focus on how the ocean levels will rise because of the melting of the polar ice-caps and all the glaciers. That's a very serious problem—can you imagine the logistics of moving coastal cities like New York, San Francisco, and Chicago a few miles inland?—but it's not the biggest immediate problem associated with the oceans.

The warmer the air is over the oceans, the more water vapor the air can hold. The warmer the water, the more of it evaporates.

public believed it was the hole in the ozone layer that was causing global warming. And a December 2010 comment on the conservative website *American Thinker* revealed just how much some people had managed to get the issues muddled:

> You know, it is actually interesting that one comment mentioned the ozone hole that we were all warned about having catastrophic consequences by the Greenies: I'm not an Ivy league educated scientist . . . but if the greenhouse gases that are supposedly so hazardous are gathering in the atmosphere and warming the planet, why wouldn't they exit through that giant hole they swore up and down existed? You can't have both. Either there is a hole, or the gases are trapped. Time for them to make up their mind.

And, obviously, the more water vapor there is in the air, the more there is of it ready to condense into liquid or solid forms when the circumstances are right, and the heavier downpours and snowfalls are likely to be.

Snowfalls are a serious problem: They can kill people. But catastrophic rainfalls are far worse. They create not just floods but mudslides, both of which claim many lives every year. They also destroy crops, which means people starve to death.

It's already happening. It's getting worse.

And as for the "global cooling" the bloviators were talking about in early 2014?

It turned out that January 2014 was, globally, the hottest January since 2007 and the fourth hottest since records began in 1880.[1] And hardly had the eastern seaboard's cold-snap ended than signs emerged that 2014's El Niño was set to be a record-breaker. So did the TV bloviators reverse course and start talking about the warming planet?

WHY IS THE CLIMATE CHANGING?

In 1824, the French physicist Joseph Fourier realized the earth was warmer than it should be. He calculated the amount of energy arriving from the sun and found it wasn't enough to give us the surface temperatures we normally enjoy. Some of his attempts to explain this were wide of the target—one was that the stars might be contributing the extra warmth—but his proposal that the atmosphere was acting like a blanket was a bullseye. Remember, a blanket works not because it keeps the cold out but because it keeps the warmth *in*.

By about the middle of the nineteenth century, the existence of the atmospheric greenhouse effect had been well established. The UK physicist John Tyndall did considerable work on it; he believed it was the water vapor in the atmosphere that trapped heat. Later in the century, the Swedish physicist Svante Arrhenius identified atmospheric carbon

---

1. Information from the National Climatic Data Center of the National Oceanic and Atmospheric Administration (NOAA).

dioxide (CO_2) as a major contributor to the greenhouse effect, and calculated fairly accurately the relationship between CO_2 levels and global temperatures. We now know that the important atmospheric gases involved in the greenhouse effect—the *greenhouse gases*—are water vapor (H_2O), carbon dioxide (CO_2), and methane (CH_4). They're not just important for climate change, let's remember: Without them, the earth would be about 60 Fahrenheit degrees colder than it is and thus pretty hostile to human life.

The way the greenhouse effect works is that energy arrives at the earth's surface in the form of sunlight; by the time it has bounced around down here and been used for things like fueling evolution (see page 87), it's mainly in the form of longer-wave radiation—infrared, or heat. While the shorter-wavelength light didn't have much trouble penetrating the atmosphere on the way in, the longer-wavelength infrared energy has some difficulty escaping back out into space. This is because the greenhouse gases, which couldn't absorb much of the incoming light, are able to absorb far more of the infrared energy. When they emit that heat again they do so in all directions, including back down toward the surface.

The net result is that a balance is struck whereby the surface of the earth is kept at temperatures in which, for the most part, we can survive.[1]

The atmospheric greenhouse effect is, then, something that science has known about for well over a century and a half. That's a lot longer than we've known why planes can fly, that atoms are made up of smaller

---

1. Confusingly, actual greenhouses stay warm primarily for a rather different reason. The air inside them is warmed by the sunlight but is then unable to mix with cooler air, which is what would happen if it weren't enclosed.

"CO$_2$ DOESN'T LEAD, IT LAGS"

Another climate change denialist cliche. The claim here is that research-es of past warming episodes have shown that the rise in CO$_2$ *follows* the warming, rather than precedes it. We've therefore got things back to front if we think rising CO$_2$ levels are going to warm the planet. What *really* happens, they say, is that *the warming causes the CO$_2$ buildup*!

We see here an example of an initial misunderstanding of genuine science becoming enshrined in the denialists' script despite—as is so often the case—the error having been pointed out countless times.

Ice ages are made up of a series of very cold periods (glacials) inter-spersed by warmer ones (interglacials). For the past few thousand years we've been living in an interglacial of the so-called Pleistocene ice age.

particles, or that ours isn't the only galaxy in the universe. Our under-standing of the greenhouse effect has now advanced to the point where we can study its workings on other planets.

It's thus astonishing that some climate change denialists believe—more likely, pretend to believe—that the greenhouse effect doesn't exist, or at least that there's some doubt about it. For example, the journalist Peter Hitchens, a prominent climate change denialists, wrote in 2001 that "The greenhouse effect probably doesn't exist. There is as yet no evidence for it." He is, alas, far from alone in his ignorance of this as-pect of basic science.

Ever since the dawn of the Industrial Revolution in Europe in the latter half of the eighteenth century, and its spread to other parts of

Were it not for manmade global warming, this interglacial would probably have ended in another few thousand years.

What happens toward the end of a glacial period is that some external influence—probably a minor shift in the earth's orbit—initiates warming. This is very slow at first. Gradually the oceans warm. Warm water holds less CO_2 in solution than cold water can, so CO_2 starts being released into the atmosphere. This builds up and then, through the greenhouse effect, completes the rest of the warming—the other 90 percent or so.

In other words, you have here an example of feedback at work: a small warming triggers the release of CO_2, and then the CO_2 is responsible for the bulk of the warming.

the world, humankind has been pumping greater and greater amounts of greenhouse gases into the atmosphere. Partly this is because of the increased reliance on burning fossil fuels like coal, oil, and natural gas. Partly it's because of a rapidly rising population. Clearly the two factors are intertwined.

This addition of greenhouse gases to the atmosphere is the prime cause of the current global warming. There is no reasonable scientific doubt about it. Climate scientists have made predictions (those "computer models" the bloviators so often sneer at) based on various increases of atmospheric greenhouse gas concentrations, and those predictions have been generally borne out.

It is certainly conceivable that there may be other factors that are contributing to climate change in a minor way, but the overwhelming cause—and the only one we're in a position to do anything about—is human activity.

A COMPLICIT MEDIA

Almost 98 percent of the world's climate scientists agree that drastic climate change is imminent, and indeed already underway, and that the primary cause of this impending catastrophe is human activity— principally the burning of fossil fuels such as coal (in power stations) and oil (in motor vehicles, machinery, central heating, et cetera). Just over 2 percent of the world's climate scientists disagree—and that includes those who're directly employed by the fossil fuel industries or indirectly employed by them through the "think tanks" those industries fund.

So you'd expect the news media to give 98 percent of the coverage to established science and just 2 percent to the denialists, right?

Wrong, of course.

A major problem with modern news media is, as we've seen, the quest for "balance"—which all too often leads to *false* balance. Even the website of the BBC, which prides itself on being among the world's most impartial news sources, for some years felt bound to give climate "skeptics" nearly the same space as climate scientists.

Some news sources go far further than this. In the US, the *Wall Street Journal* and, of course, Fox News and CNBC have mounted what's often called a War on Science in the arena of climate change, while the *Washington Post* makes a feature of the views of its denialist contributor George F. Will. Since early 2012, Reuter's, under deputy editor-in-chief and now managing editor Paul Ingrassia, a proud "climate skeptic," has both radically decreased its climate coverage and increased its use of false balance as a means of promoting anti-science. In the UK, the *Mail* and *Telegraph* newspapers trumpet contributors who regularly attack the science and the Intergovernmental Panel on Climate Change (IPCC), often displaying quite astonishing levels of viciousness and scientific illiteracy; it's hard to believe this can be anything other than a deliberate campaign by the editors of those papers to delay action on climate change. In Australia, the *Melbourne Herald Sun* and *The Australian* similarly give prominence to denialist contributors. Many of these news outlets belong, as does Fox News, to Rupert Murdoch; ironically, Murdoch has stated outright that there's a climate change crisis, so it appears he doesn't read or watch his own media.

Another way to skew the debate is simply to reduce the news coverage of climate issues so that the public is lulled into a false sense of security. In 2012, the Discovery Channel aired a seven-hour series called *Frozen Planet* about the plight of the earth's poles and included not a word of explanation as to why the ice is melting. Overall, news coverage of climate issues has been plummeting; in 2011 the TV channels ABC, CBS, NBC, and Fox spent less than half the time discussing climate change that they did talking about Donald Trump!

"THE CLIMATE HAS CHANGED BEFORE"

It has indeed, and the causes have been various.

The world's climate changed drastically about 66 million years ago, almost certainly because of the impact of the large asteroid or cometary nucleus that created what is now called the Chicxulub crater in the Gulf of Mexico. The impact hurled a huge mass of dust and other detritus high into the atmosphere, where it blocked off the rays of the sun. This caused a worldwide "winter" that lasted many years. With plants unable to photosynthesize, food would have been in drastically short supply. About three-quarters of the earth's living species, including almost all the dinosaurs except the winged ones (which would evolve into birds), went extinct.

The dinosaurs had been around for over 150 million years and had dominated life on land for most of that time. This was no minor extinction. By comparison, we've been around just a few million years and came to our position of dominance mere thousands of years ago.

Luckily for us, the climate change that the world is experiencing isn't as sudden as the one that exterminated the dinosaurs. We still have a chance, not to stop it, but to lessen its worst effects. That's the good news. The bad news is that its results are likely to be very much longer-lasting. The greenhouse gases that we've been producing will remain in the atmosphere for centuries.

Other major episodes of climate change have been the various ice ages. We know the earth has experienced at least five of these, during which for millions of years the planet's surface temperature is lower than usual, there are major icecaps at the poles, and glaciers cover much of the land.

A far milder and more short-lived episode was the so-called Little Ice Age, which affected Europe from about the middle of the fourteenth century to about the middle of the nineteenth.[1] No one's exactly

---

1. Climatologists disagree about the start and end dates of the Little Ice Age, so you'll likely find different ones stated elsewhere.

VENUS—WHAT A RUNAWAY GREENHOUSE EFFECT LOOKS LIKE

C.S. Lewis, author of the *Chronicles of Narnia*, also wrote some science fiction. One of his SF novels, *Perelandra* (1943)—sometimes called *Voyage to Venus*—depicts a journey to what was then thought to be a sort of sister world to ours. Although closer to the sun than the earth is, Venus is about the same size and, as people knew by the 1940s, has a thick, cloudy atmosphere. So Lewis portrayed Venus as a world much like earth, though warmer, and with a surface that's mainly ocean. The atmosphere is breathable; sunlight can penetrate it, although the disk of the sun is hidden by the cloud cover.

What we didn't discover until much later is that Venus is in the grip of a runaway greenhouse effect from which it will likely never escape. The planet's atmosphere is mainly CO_2. This atmosphere is very thick: Its pressure is about the same as what you'd experience if you were roughly a half-mile underwater. The temperature is about 750°F—far hotter than a kitchen oven—and so the rocks on the surface are literally red hot. Those thick clouds contain sulfur dioxide, and they rain sulfuric acid.

It's extremely unlikely that, no matter how much CO_2 we add to the atmosphere, the earth will become another Venus—if only because, long before we could add enough CO_2, we'd be entirely wiped out. But it is possible that, because of feedback, our activities could cause the planet to suffer a runaway greenhouse effect after our species's demise.

sure what caused this cooling (perhaps a glitch in the Gulf Stream, the Atlantic ocean current that washes warm water against northwestern Europe?), but it does seem to have been localized to that region. There were some other coolings around the world at intervals during this same period, but it's not certain they were directly related.

The cooling involved in the Little Ice Age was by a couple of Fahrenheit degrees, and was confined to just part of the globe. That's not much by comparison with the kind of temperature *increase* we're facing, which will be worldwide.

When we look at the several periods when there were major extinctions of life on earth, we find they seem all to be associated in some way with climate change. The massive volcanic events (basalt flood events) that occasionally shake the earth can exterminate life directly by flooding huge areas with lava, but their aftermath sees the death of many more species because of climate change. Periods when the upper levels of the oceans are deprived of oxygen (are anoxic), so that all sorts of marine creatures can't live there, can have various causes but again are likely to be associated with climate change.[1]

How serious a problem is this? After the Permian extinction some 250 million years ago, it took life perhaps 10 million years to recover—and some estimates go as high as 50 million years.

The short lesson is: You really, really don't want to be around when climate change happens.

Unfortunately, we don't have much choice in that.

A recurring theme among climate change denialists is that, since

---

1. At the moment we're exacerbating this problem by destroying ocean life in various other ways, such as pollution and overfishing.

we weren't around during previous major episodes of climate change, and certainly weren't burning fossil fuels at the time, why should we be worried now?

That really requires a two-part answer:

1. Not all periods of climate change are brought on by the same cause or group of causes. This is hardly surprising. You fall sick for various reasons, not the same one every time. We do know that pouring vast amounts of greenhouse gases into the atmosphere is one way of causing global warming. That's really all that's relevant.

2. It *doesn't matter* what caused those other climate changes. The only one that affects our survival is the one that's happening now. Since we know that our production of greenhouse gases through fossil fuel burning is the primary cause this time around, and since we're in a position to *do* something about it, we should be doing that something—not fiddling while the world burns.

"THERE HASN'T BEEN ANY WARMING SINCE 1998!"

When we talk about global warming, we usually talk about the atmosphere—after all, that's where the greenhouse gases that we're pumping out are accumulating, and that's where those greenhouse gases are do-

"BUT THE ANTARCTIC'S GAINING ICE!"

For once a climate change denialist claim that isn't entirely baloney—just hopelessly misleading.

The ocean surrounding the continent of Antarctica builds up an ice covering every winter, most of which melts during the summer. This is a regular annual event and thus has little effect on year-on-year global sea levels. For reasons that aren't fully understood—they may be connected with the hole in the ozone layer over the south pole—at the moment there's more *sea* ice forming in winter than is melting in summer.

But sea ice is a very minor player in terms of the Antarctic ice as a whole. Most of the Antarctic's ice is locked up in the "permanent" ice sheet that has accumulated on the continental landmass over millions of years. At the moment, this ice sheet is melting at a rapidly increasing rate. (The same is happening in the northern hemisphere to the ice sheet that covers Greenland.) It's this far bigger melting that's the problem.

The melting isn't uniform all over the continent. There's actually a slight buildup of the ice sheet going on in eastern Antarctica. This gain, however, is outstripped by the losses of ice elsewhere. The denialists are in effect cherry picking by looking solely at eastern Antarctica and forgetting about the rest.

ing the damage. But measurements of atmospheric temperatures aren't necessarily the best way of keeping tabs on warming. Short-term climate variations, such as El Niño/La Niña years, can affect the picture—

not in any way that climate scientists can't take account of, but in ways that climate change denialists seize upon only too eagerly.

Because the oceans are so much more massive than the atmosphere, they respond much less sensitively to short-term variations. Modern measurements of global temperatures take into account what's happening not just to the atmosphere (upper as well as lower) but also the oceans.

This renders moot the arguments by the prominent climate change denialist Anthony Watts and others that land-based meteorological stations are sited such as to show greater warming than is really going on. If weather satellites, whether surveying the land or the oceans, all tell the same story as the ground-based stations, it's clear there's no real problem with the ground-based reports.

Measurements of the rise in global surface temperatures currently show an average rise of about 0.2 Fahrenheit degrees per decade. That doesn't seem like much, except that a decade isn't long when you're talking about a global climate regime. Similarly, it isn't long when you're talking about the glacial speed with which the world's politicians can be persuaded to *do* anything to avert the imminent crisis. Remember, the George W. Bush administration's charade in 2000 that the "science wasn't yet in" on climate change held up US efforts for the lifetime of that administration plus a few further years. A decade or more wasted just like that.

A further point to note is that surface temperatures in the Arctic are currently rising at a faster rate than the average. This is having the effect of melting the permafrost—those enormous tracts of land, primarily in Siberia but also in northern North America, Greenland, et cetera., where the ground is frozen solid all year round.

Or, at least, it used to be. After over 10,000 years, it's melting. As it melts it's releasing huge amounts of methane that were, in effect, frozen in. Methane is an even more effective greenhouse gas than CO_2. The danger is obvious. If something isn't done pronto about the warming we're already experiencing, and the permafrost melts completely to release its entire consignment of methane, we may be in for a far rougher ride than even the dourest pessimist could have predicted a couple of decades ago.

An interesting side effect of the permafrost melting is that trapped viruses are also escaping. In January 2014, a team of French scientists announced the discovery in the permafrost of a virus that had lain dormant for 30,000 years but that was, on thawing out, infectious again. That virus, *Pithovirus sibericum*, isn't infectious to humans, but who knows what other bugs may soon become reactivated? "[T]he thawing of permafrost either from global warming or industrial exploitation of circumpolar regions," they said, "might not be exempt from future threats to human or animal health."

Let's get back to that claim about the earth having cooled since 1998.

Since annual mean atmospheric temperatures are rising not in a straight line or smooth curve but in a zigzag, it's easy to find an unusually hot year and then make a big song and dance about later years that are cooler. This is a classic example of cherry picking data (see page 48), and it's a practice the climate change denialists have exploited to the hilt.

Yes, 1998 was an exceptionally hot year, the hottest ever to that date and still the third hottest on record. The denialists made much noise about "cooling" thereafter . . . until 2005, which turned out to be, oops, even hotter. And then 2010 came along, and it was hotter still. In fact, nine of the ten warmest years ever recorded have been since 2002, the other one being 1998.

"BUT IT'S NOT THAT LONG AGO THAT SCIENTISTS WERE PREDICTING AN ICE AGE!"

They were?

It's a claim you often hear voiced by climate change denialists. For example, writing in the *Washington Times* in February 2014, Joseph Curl refers his readers to a 1971 *Washington Post* article headlined "U.S. Scientist Sees New Ice Age Coming" and extracts from it the following scary quote: "The world could be as little as 50 or 60 years away from a disastrous new ice age, a leading atmospheric scientist predicts." What Curl must have assumed is that none of his readers would go look up the article concerned, a breathless piece by journalist Victor Cohn about some research being done on aerosols by scientists S.I. Rasool and Steve Schneider on the effect that big increases of human-made aerosols in the atmosphere could have on the earth's climate. They reported that these could cause cooling if trends continued and if no other factors were involved.[1] But other factors *were* involved—factors

---

1. They were right, by the way. Between about 1945 and the mid-1970s there was a pause in global warming because the air pollution we were creating caused a rise in atmospheric sulfate aerosols. Just before you think that going back to massive air pollution could be the answer to global warming, remember that—aside from all the people who die as a direct consequence of air pollution—those sulfates produce acid rain, which in turn causes large-scale deforestation (thereby exacerbating global warming) and kills off the upper levels of the oceans . . . where our food supply comes from.

THE HOCKEY STICK

One of the most-disputed diagrams in human history must be the famous Hockey Stick graph.

The first version was produced in 1998 by the US climatologist Michael Mann and his colleagues Raymond Bradley and Malcolm Hughes. Using newly developed statistical methods, they plotted global temperatures from the year 1400 up to the present. The resulting graph was roughly horizontal along most of its width before turning upward steeply at its right-hand side, representing the most recent past. It was because of this shape that it got the Hockey Stick nickname. Later versions of the graph, incorporating huge amounts of extra data from far more sources than were available to Mann and the others in 1998, show a strikingly similar shape. As do a string of independent assessments of the data. While, as in every aspect of climate science, there can be argument over the details—notably over some of the earlier sections of the temperature history—there's absolutely no doubt that the picture

like the greenhouse gases, whose possible role in future climate change had barely begun to be appreciated.

Worse still, you'll often find the name of James Hansen associated with that 1971 story, as if he'd been working in association with Rasool and Schneider. Since Hansen is one of the world's most prominent scientists warning of the dangers of climate change, this might seem like big news.

Except that it isn't true.

offered by the Hockey Stick graph is a real one.

In 2005, however, a retired mining prospector called Steve Mc-Intyre did his own reanalysis of the data. He was helped in getting this into print in the journal *Geophysical Research Letters* by an economist called Ross McKitrick; the latter has been associated with fossil fuel industry-funded "think tanks" like the Heartland Institute. Their claim that Mann and his colleagues seriously distorted the data and that there's nothing to worry about was picked up by the denialist camp and the media . . . none of whom seemed to notice that neither McIntyre nor McKitrick is professionally qualified to judge matters of climate science. Once again, we're being asked to believe you'd be better off having a plumber operate on your brain than a brain surgeon.

Because of the vicious hate campaign mounted by the climate-change deniers, Mann has received death threats, faced persecution through the courts by Virginia's (now mercifully former) Attorney General, the denialist Ken Cuccinelli, and been libeled in the press.

Hansen started out as a NASA planetary scientist. He didn't get involved in climate change until 1976, five years after Cohn's article was published in the *Post*. Hansen's involvement was to lend Rasool and Schneider a program he'd written and found useful when studying the atmosphere of Venus.

Other references cited by the climate change denialists as supposed "proof" of the scientists' flip-flop include a 1975 *Newsweek* article by Peter Gwynne called "The Cooling World" and a 1977 cover of *Time* magazine showing a photo of a handsome penguin over the strapline "How to Survive the Coming Ice Age." The problem with the *Time* cover is that it's a phony, faked up in PhotoShop. The photographic part of it is from a 2007 *Time* cover where the strapline reads: "The Global Warming Survival Guide."

The fact is that in the 1970s there *were* some climate scientists worried about the possibility of global cooling. However, even at the time they were in a fairly small minority. In 2008, Thomas Peterson of the National Climatic Data Center surveyed the relevant scientific papers produced between 1965 and 1979 and found that 62 percent of them predicted warming, 28 percent took no position on the matter, and just 10 percent were worried about cooling.

Since then, further researches—and a greater number of years over which to establish patterns—have changed the picture a bit, until now, as we know, nearly 98 percent of climate scientists are concerned about warming and almost no one's concerned about cooling.

The reason? All the extra evidence that's been gathered since 1980.

That's the way science works. We get closer and closer to the truth.

"THE REASON THE ATMOSPHERE'S GETTING HOTTER IS BECAUSE THE SUN'S GETTING HOTTER"

One step up from the people who claim climate change isn't happening—and that all those extreme weather events don't count—are the ones who admit that climate change is real but claim it *isn't our fault*.

A frequent argument is that the real driver of global warming has nothing to do with greenhouse gases. It's that the sun's getting hotter.

The sun *does* vary a little in its energy output, and at the moment it *is* slightly warmer than usual. But the increase in the sun's temperature is very tiny, and we could expect its effect on the earth's climate to be minuscule.

Even so, scientists have checked to make sure it isn't the culprit. The innermost level of the earth's atmosphere is called the troposphere. It's in the troposphere that clouds form, birds fly, and we live. It's also in the troposphere that greenhouse gases like carbon dioxide build up—in other words, it's in this lowest region of the atmosphere that climate change is happening.

Above the troposphere lies the stratosphere. There are other layers of atmosphere above the stratosphere, with the air getting thinner and thinner. Unless you're an atmospheric scientist or an astronaut, it's kind of hard to tell the difference between these upper layers and outer space.

In order to reach us, energy arriving from the sun has to pass through these thin outermost layers, then the stratosphere, and finally the troposphere.

So the stratosphere's warmed directly by the energy that's arriving from the sun, and it's warmed a bit more by the energy that's reflecting back up from the surface. It's not difficult to see that, if global warming was just a matter of the sun getting hotter, the stratosphere would be getting hotter along with everything else.

In fact, the opposite is true. Because more than usual of the energy that comes up from the surface is getting trapped in the troposphere by the greenhouse gases there, the stratosphere is actually *cooling down a little.*[1] Here's a graph of stratosphere temperatures from the National Climatic Data Center:

The different lines show different sets of data drawn from different sources. It's obvious that the results are all virtually identical.

The stratosphere is not only cooling, it's cooling in exactly the way that computer climate models predicted we would find. Although a few scientists believe there's evidence the sun's contribution to global warming is more than tiny, even they agree that the main cause is the

---

1. There's a further complicating factor: Ozone in the stratosphere traps some of the ultraviolet radiation arriving from the sun, and this warms up the air around it. The damage done to the ozone layer during the twentieth century (see page 188) had the side effect of cooling down the stratosphere. The ozone layer is slowly recovering, but it still has a way to go. Atmospheric scientists obviously take this into account.

generation of greenhouse gases by our burning of fossil fuels.

Almost the only people who disagree are some media bloviators and some politicians. Well, in a sense they're experts on hot gases, too . . .

"WE SHOULD BE WELCOMING GLOBAL WARMING!"

In 2009, Representative John Shimkus told the House Energy and Commerce Committee's Energy and Environment Subcommittee:

> If we decrease the use of carbon dioxide are we not taking away plant food from the atmosphere? We could be doing just the opposite of what the people who want to save the world are saying. . . . Today we have 388 parts per million in the atmosphere. I believe in the days of the dinosaurs, where we had the most flora and fauna, we were probably at 4,000 parts per million. There is a theological debate that this is a carbon-starved planet, not too much carbon.

What theology has to do with climate change is a bit of a mystery, but the other two elements of what Shimkus said are common themes of climate change denialists.

Plants, as we all know, take in CO_2 and release oxygen (O_2). In that sense, CO_2 can certainly be considered to be plant food. This has led some denialists to wonder why conservationists wring their hands about deforestation while at the same time begging people to reduce

CLIMATE CHANGE—LEFT OR RIGHT?

Often climate change is presented—at least in the US—as a political issue, a battleground between left and right. The stereotype is that liberals accept climate science and are urgent to take action to mitigate the situation while conservatives either disbelieve (or don't know) the scientific evidence or are more concerned about short-term profits than the survival of their children and grandchildren.

That may have been true once, but today it has become a caricature.

Certainly it's true that the vast majority of those *politicians* who refuse to do anything about climate change and who belittle climate science are to the right of center, but, more and more, ordinary people of every political persuasion are recognizing that we're facing perhaps the biggest crisis our species has ever had to face . . . and that the crisis is getting more desperate with every passing day that we do nothing.

A poll published in February 2014 by Harstad Strategic Research, commissioned by the National Resources Defense Council (NRDC), shows this new political reality. The pollsters questioned people in four red states (Louisiana, Alaska, Arkansas, North Carolina) and five blue or purple states (Iowa, Michigan, Virginia, Colorado, New Hampshire). Although the majorities in favor of action on climate change are not as big in the red states as they are in the blue/purple states, they're still comfortably greater than 2:1. And, while Democrats are far more likely than independents and Republicans to want action, even the latter support the relevant measures by a very clear majority.[1]

---

1. The percentages in favor/don't know/opposed are: Democrats 87/5/8, independents 63/7/30 and Republicans 53/8/39.

the amount of CO_2 they pump into the atmosphere. Surely the answer is to *increase* our CO_2 output, not reduce it?

The trouble is that, as was known years before Shimkus made his claim, plants can stand only a certain concentration of CO_2 in the air around them before the air becomes, as it were, too rich for them: Far from flourishing, the plants suffer. So the idea that you can make plants healthier by dosing them with more and more CO_2 is akin to the old mistake that, if one beer makes you happy, twenty beers will make you *very* happy.

There are other, less direct reasons why increasing atmospheric CO_2 concentrations won't help agriculture; for example, one consequence of the extra CO_2 would be more ozone (O_3) at ground level—bad news for plants. And most obvious of all is the point that you need just a few days of blisteringly hot temperatures, such as you might expect in a warmed world, to devastate your crops entirely.

The whole misguided notion that building up ever more CO_2 in the atmosphere will make the earth a green and bounteous planet can be traced back to a video called *The Greening of Planet Earth*. Released in 1991 under the cover of a front group, Greening Earth Society, this was in fact a propaganda exercise funded by Western Fuels Association, a coal company. Entirely missing from the video was consideration of any of the downsides of global warming. Even so, at the time people were innocent enough to think the energy corporations wouldn't go so far as to flat-out lie to us.

During the Jurassic period, the heyday of the dinosaurs, atmospheric CO_2 levels were probably around 2,000 parts per million.[1] While

---

1. The further into the past you go, the more difficult it obviously becomes to determine atmospheric compositions accurately.

that's a long way from 4,000 parts per million, it's obviously very much higher than the CO_2 levels we're worried about today. At the same time, however, the earth was cooler, because the sun was then less bright. (The slow brightening of the sun over the past 150 million years or so does *not* account for the sudden upturn in global temperatures over the past few decades.) The atmosphere could support far higher CO_2 levels without things going haywire precisely because there was less energy coming in from the sun.

In these circumstances there was indeed luxuriant plant growth, upon which the herbivorous dinosaurs could feast . . . only to be feasted upon themselves by the predatory dinosaurs, of course. Much of the planet was a hothouse.

The point to remember is one that should be obvious even to politicians like John Shimkus:

WE'RE

NOT

DINOSAURS!

Well, most of us aren't, anyway.

What's forgotten in all those science fiction stories about people going back in time to visit the dinosaurs is that the world the dinosaurs lived in was one we would find really quite inimical to our survival. Despite the cooler sun, the heat was intense and the humidity likewise. The high CO_2 concentration in the air, alongside all the rest—including, it's thought, oxygen levels lower than those we're accustomed to—would make breathing a nightmare for our intrepid time travelers.

With the planet now bathed by a hotter sun, CO_2 levels won't need to build up to anything like 2,000 parts per million to achieve similar conditions to those the dinosaurs enjoyed. Given enough time—in other words, a slow increase in temperatures and CO_2 levels over many thousands of years—humans and other modern plants and animals could adapt until they flourished in those conditions.

But not in a matter of decades.

THE ECONOMICS OF CLIMATE CHANGE

In 2004 the writer and movie director Michael Crichton, best known for *Jurassic Park* (1990), published a novel called *State of Fear*. The plot saw environmentalists committing terrorist acts to persuade the world of the threat of global warming, and other environmentalists who know global warming's just a hoax facilitating the criminal activities in order to maintain their sources of funding. Crichton, who decades before had trained as a physician, presented impressive-looking charts and so on to give unsuspecting readers the impression he knew what he was talking about when it came to climate change.

As climate scientists were quick to point out, Crichton was in fact about as authoritative on climate science as they themselves were on medicine.

Basing a thriller novel on a conspiracy theory is nothing new, whether the novelist uses an existing conspiracy theory or invents one out of thin air. Astonishingly, though, some readers took his invented conspiracy theory seriously. Presumably those same people believe it's possible to recreate living dinosaurs by cloning DNA from dinosaur

"IT'S NOT WORTH DOING ANYTHING UNTIL INDIA AND CHINA GET THEIR ACT TOGETHER"

This is the infantile "I'm not going to stop pooping in *my* pants until *he* stops pooping in *his* pants" argument—and it's not even based on genuine information.

According to the World Bank's figures, in 2010 the rate of CO_2 emissions (metric tons per capita) was

- 1.7 in India
- 6.2 in China
- 7.9 in the UK
- 16.9 in Australia
- 17.6 in the US

blood in a fossil mosquito.

A prime figure among those who support the conspiracy theory that climate change is just a hoax mounted by climate scientists eager to perpetuate their research funding is Senator James Inhofe: "With all of the hysteria, all of the fear, all of the phony science, could it be that man-made global warming is the greatest hoax ever perpetrated on the American people? It sure sounds like it," he said in the Senate in July 2003. He has repeated this claim often.

Inhofe was Chairman of the Senate's Environment and Public Works Committee 2003–06, and through that position he played a

Remind me, again, just which are the countries that should be getting their act together?

The US wasn't the worst in the World Bank's table—look to Kuwait, Trinidad & Tobago, and Qatar for that dubious "honor"—but it fared pretty shamefully.

There's one more point. Imagine you've been held up, and by the time you reach home everyone else has had dinner already: There's only your plate of food left. Would you think it was fair if the rest of the family insisted everyone get an equal share of that plateful?

No. Of course you wouldn't. You'd point out that the other folks had already *had* their share.

Well, that's the position the developing countries are in. The rich industrial nations have already used up their "allocation" of greenhouse gas emission. It's only reasonable that they should be the ones making the biggest effort to cut back now.

major role in ensuring that for years, at least in the US, little or nothing was done about mercury pollution, which he had decided was no real health problem. He was similarly diligent in stomping efforts to deter climate change—so diligent, in fact, that it was sometimes hard to understand his motives. That was until information started coming out about the size of the "campaign contributions" Inhofe was receiving from the fossil fuel and energy industries.

Another to swallow the conspiracy theory whole and to explain the economic case against doing anything has been Sarah Palin. She spelled out the science of it all to the Southern Republican Leadership

Conference in April 2010:

> We should create a competitive climate for investment
> and for renewables and alternatives that are economi-
> cal and doable and none of this snake oil science stuff
> that is based on this global warming, Gore-gate stuff that
> came down where there was revelation that the scientists,
> some of these scientists were playing political games.

Speaking to the broadcaster Rachel Maddow in 2012, James Inhofe admitted that his campaign to smear climate science and climate scientists
began not from any belief in a conspiracy theory:

> I was actually on your side of this issue when . . . I first
> heard about this. I thought it must be true until I found
> out what it cost.

In other words, he opposes taking action on climate change for economic reasons. All of the rest of his claims about it being a hoax are
just hogwash.

Hmmm. Treating cancer is difficult and expensive, so let's all say
cancer is just a hoax invented by the medical profession!

The bizarre thing about the conspiracy theory is that the real way
to make money out of climate change is in climate change *denial*. If
you look at all the journalists who're promoting the denialist bullshit—
James Delingpole, Christopher Booker, George F. Will, Andrew Bolt,
and countless others—they're almost without exception earning pay
paychecks of a size to make even prominent climate scientists wistful.

The few scientists who've sold out to denialist "think tanks" are being healthily paid to promote the denial—money for nothing, you might think, because they don't have to do any research.

No one pretends that shifting our society from fossil fuel reliance to renewable energy sources like solar power is going to be easy, or that the transition isn't going to involve some large-scale investment. Yet plenty of countries and corporations are finding the investment makes sense not just environmentally, but also economically.

A further economic point is that, while the transition to a climate-friendly economy may cost money, failing to do anything about climate change costs even more. In 2009, the International Energy Agency estimated that each year we delay taking action on climate change will cost us $500 billion later on. The longer we put off doing anything, the bigger the crisis—and the bigger the final bill.

The biggest economic cost of all, of course, will be if we put things off so long that it becomes *impossible* to put things right. Who can calculate the economic costs of a collapsed civilization?

Climate change denialists say this disaster won't happen, so anything spent on averting climate change is money down the drain. They're like people who're told the road has subsided just round the next corner, but who carry on driving at 90 MPH anyway, because "who knows until you get there?"

Let's imagine for a moment that somehow, impossibly, all the world's climate scientists—or the "warming alarmists," to use the denialists' jargon—have gotten it wrong. We spend a lot of money switching to renewable energy sources like solar power and then discover it was something we needn't have done. Just how bad would this situation be?

After the initial investment had been written off, energy would be cheaper and the world would be a cleaner, healthier, better place to live in.

How bad is that?

🚫

6. THAT ISN'T EXACTLY HOW IT WENT: FAKING HISTORY

9/11: INVENTING THE IMMEDIATE PAST

In the months and years after the September 11, 2001 terrorist attacks, conspiracy theories galore grew up claiming, among much else, that

- it wasn't a plane that struck the Pentagon but a cruise missile,
- the World Trade Center buildings couldn't have collapsed of their own accord but must have been demolished by bombs planted inside them, and
- the whole operation was carried out not by al-Qaeda but as a false flag operation by the George W. Bush administration, seeking to boost Bush's flagging popularity and find an excuse to invade Iraq for oil.

The conspiracy theorists created a noise machine that convinced many people that there "must be something in" their ideas. As so often happens, quieter, more sober voices tended to get drowned out. Once the dust settled, it was realized that there was no real reason to doubt the explanation of events that had been offered from the outset.

The Bush administration didn't help matters by piling on further untruths. It did indeed use the 9/11 attacks as an excuse for invading Iraq, claiming that Iraq's leader, Saddam Hussein, had been behind the plot; in fact, the secular Saddam Hussein regime and the religious-fundamentalist al-Qaeda were bitter enemies.[1] Great efforts were made to cover up the fact that President Bush, in person, had been warned beforehand that a terrorist attack was coming down the pike and had done nothing about it. Administration hawks like Vice-President Dick Cheney and Secretary of Defense Donald Rumsfeld claimed Iraq was nursing stockpiles of weapons of mass destruction (WMDs) even though, largely ignored by the US news media, teams of UN weapons inspectors, on the ground in Iraq, were reporting no such stockpiles. Led by Hans Blix, the weapons inspectors eventually left the country for safety reasons just before the US invasion; later George W. Bush would claim that one reason for the invasion was that Hussein had been refusing to let the weapons inspectors into the country. In fact, no WMDs were ever found; as Blix's team and Hussein himself had said, he had destroyed his stockpiles years earlier.

We all have a tendency to fake history, whether it's "the dog ate my homework" or spinning anecdotes to make yourself look good. We expect our politicians to do some "embroidering" of history, from covering up their scandals to exaggerating the contribution they made to decisions now seen as good ones; of course, we don't—and shouldn't—expect our government to fake history on a grand scale in order to take our country into war.

We all have a tendency, too, to indulge in conspiracy theories of history, on a large scale or small. Remember the conspiracy theories about President Obama's birthplace (see page 25).

---

1. On occasion, of course, two bitterest enemies can temporarily collude against a third. There has never been the slightest hint that it happened in this case.

And far too many of us have a tendency to fake history in order to promote one ideology or another. As a quick example, in March 2014, after the first episode of Neil deGrasse Tyson's *Cosmos: A Spacetime Odyssey*, Joseph Farah of *World Net Daily*, a far-right webzine that's ideologically opposed to science, naturally produced a hit-piece.[1] In part this read:

> In a recent radio interview, Tyson made this statement, which would be a surprise to scientists from Isaac Newton to George Washington Carver: "If you start using your scripture, your religious text as a source of your science, that's where you run into problems. There is no example of someone reading their scripture and saying 'I have a prediction about the world that no one knows yet because this gave me insight. Let's go test this prediction and have that theory turn out to be correct.'" In fact, that is precisely what those two gentlemen did—as well as many other accomplished scientists who made world-changing discoveries rather than serve as media stars.

The history-faking is fairly obvious. While both Newton and Carver were practicing Christians—and Carver a very committed one—neither of them used the Bible as a source for his scientific theories. (Newton used the Bible as a source during his doomed researches into occultism, et cetera., but . . .) Farah is hoping his readers, who will have

---

1. The hit-piece, "Meet Obama's Favorite Astrophysicist" (March 13, 2014), was widely circulated among the pro-science crowd for laffs.

"ANOMALIES" IN NASA'S PHOTOGRAPHS[1]

- CLAIM: The black skies shown in the lunar photographs have no stars in them: clearly, when the NASA hoaxers were setting up their studio, they forgot about the stars.

- FACT: Illuminated by the sun, the foreground was bright (as bright as at noon on earth) and so the cameras' exposure times were short—too short to show items as faint as stars.

- CLAIM: After the lander landed, there was still lunar dust nearby. Surely the blast of the lander's rockets should have blown it all away?

- FACT: Not without air, no. There was no reason for dust outside the immediate area affected by the rockets to be noticeably disturbed at all.

- CLAIM: The shadows in the lunar photographs are all wrong: There are shadows from multiple light sources, indicating the scenes must have been photographed under studio lighting.

- FACT: It's true the shadows aren't as you'd expect *if the sun were the sole light source*. But it wasn't. Other light sources provided reflected sunlight from different directions. The dust of the lunar surface is highly reflective, as were the astronauts' suits.

- CLAIM: After the astronauts planted a Stars &

---

1. Primarily derived from Phil Plait's analysis on his excellent *Bad Astronomy* website.

Stripes, the flag appeared to billow in the breeze. If this were in a vacuum, shouldn't it instead have slowly settled down around the pole?

- FACT: There's a horizontal strut holding the flag out at right angles from the pole; it's clearly visible in the photos. The brief "billowing" is the flag's response to the pole's being driven into the lunar soil.
- CLAIM: In some of the photos the crosshairs of the camera's lens seem to have been obscured by the photograph's subject—a clear indication of clumsy photographic forgery.
- FACT: Remember, these weren't digital cameras: They used film. And remember, too, that the objects being photographed were *bright*. Their brightness simply flooded the film, blotting out the thin lines of the crosshairs.
- CLAIM: Film of the ascent module lifting off showed no rocket flame.
- FACT: The rocket fuel used produces a transparent flame.

heard a thousand times that Newton was a Christian (because every creationist organization trumpets the fact), will swallow the fakery that Newton's science—optics, calculus, gravity—was based on the Bible.

In this chapter we'll look at a few examples of the different types of history-faking, starting with one of the craziest conspiracy theories.

THE MOON LANDINGS NEVER HAPPENED

According to various polls, anywhere between 6 percent and an astonishing 20 percent of the US public believes the six *Apollo* lunar landings during 1969–72 were faked by NASA. Even more astonishingly, those figures actually represent an improvement: In the months after Neil Armstrong and Buzz Aldrin walked on the moon, fully 30 percent of the US public thought it was all a hoax, that the scenes supposedly filmed on the moon were in reality staged in the remote Nevada Desert.

If this were true, it would have been the most public hoax of all time. Armstrong's "one small step for a man" moment was watched live on TV by some 600 million people.

A major difficulty NASA would have faced in mounting such a hoax would have been—strange as it may seem today, when movie special effects (SFX) can deceive even the most critical eye—that the technology simply didn't exist then to do the fakery. Movies of the era like *2001: A Space Odyssey* (1968) and *Silent Running* (1971) had great SFX of life aboard spaceships and even, briefly, on the lunar surface, that actually looked *better* than NASA's *Apollo 11* footage, but the relevant scenes, all strung together, lasted mere minutes and were hugely expensive. Even if NASA had managed to find cutting-edge SFX technicians capable of creating a days-long "live" stream, it would have cost more than the mission did . . . and that stream would have been just the first of six!

This logistical problem hasn't stopped some bullshitters from claiming the *Apollo* landings were faked by a team led by Arthur C. Clarke and Stanley Kubrick; if that was the case, Arthur told me years later, he wanted his royalties.

The initial cynicism was probably a reflection of the distrust the US public then felt toward its government. Richard Nixon had not long before been elected president with promises to wind down the Vietnam War swiftly; instead, he promptly intensified it. By 1976, when William Kaysing published the book *We Never Went to the Moon: America's Thirty Billion Dollar Swindle* (with Randy Reid), Watergate had happened and the US public was prepared to believe anything about its rulers.

Those who've followed in Kaysing's footsteps have, like him, made much of so-called "anomalies" in the photographs returned to earth by the astronauts. One "anomaly" they generally ignore is that the dust particles kicked up by the astronauts and the lunar buggy can be seen to follow a parabolic path, indicating a vacuum; had the astronauts been operating on earth, that kicked-up dust would have formed clouds. And, sticking with the dust, the conspiracy theorists fail to explain why the breeze they claim is making the flag billow isn't moving the surface dust around.

Another concern often voiced is that the astronauts couldn't have survived the dose of radiation they got as they passed through the Van Allen belts. In fact, NASA took precautionary steps to minimize the astronauts' radiation exposure.

In 2001, many of the conspiracists' concerns were brought together in a credulous Fox TV "documentary" called *Conspiracy Theory: Did We Land on the Moon?* Among the show's claims was that the technology for the *Apollo* SFX had been derived from that created for the movie *Capricorn One*. There's one big difficulty with that claim:

- The *Apollo* landings ran 1969–72.
- *Capricorn One* wasn't made until 1977.

That same year, 1977, saw the release of *A Funny Thing Happened on the Way to the Moon*, made by conspiracy theorist Bart Sibrel. The movie can be found on YouTube, as can a video of the glorious occasion in 2002 when the elderly Buzz Aldrin, after harassment from the much larger and younger Sibrel—including the brayed accusation that he was "a coward and a liar"—socked him on the jaw. It's no real way to settle a scientific argument, but then a scientific argument wasn't what Sibrel was offering.

DENYING THE HOLOCAUST

It seems beyond the bounds of credibility that anyone could say that perhaps the biggest crime of the twentieth century,[1] the Holocaust— the systematic murder of millions of Jews,[2] gays, Romanies, Serbs, et cetera.—never happened. There are the testimonies of the survivors of the death camps and of those who actually carried out the slaughter. There's photographic and forensic evidence galore, not to mention the memories of the Allied soldiers who liberated the camps. There are the Nazis' own records, showing not just the details of the extermination but also the technology whereby it was carried out. Even though many of those documents were obliterated in the later years of World War II,

---

1. Perhaps even bigger was what Josef Stalin did to the people of the USSR, not just through murder but through ideological science denial that resulted in the deaths of millions by starvation.
2. For the sake of concision, from here on I'm going to talk about the Holocaust in terms of the European Jews who died. What the Nazis did to other "degenerates" is equally painful to contemplate, and in some instances the death toll was comparable (see page 45).

we have the records of the Nazi group that carried out that obliteration: Aktion 1005, whose leader, Paul Blobel, gave the gruesome details at the Nuremberg Trials after the war.

Most significantly of all, none of the Nazis on trial at Nuremberg or later—not even Adolf Eichmann, who largely masterminded the logistics of the attempted genocide of the European Jews and who was much later captured by the Israelis, put on trial, and executed in 1961—pretended that the Holocaust didn't happen.

Yet a small but vociferous group of people claim it's all just a hoax.

One school of Holocaust deniers says Zionists invented the Holocaust after World War II as a way of maximizing the reparations they claimed from the Germans to help fund the new state of Israel.

This hypothesis has various problems. One is that the broad outlines of what had happened during the Holocaust were established fairly soon after the end of the war, whereas the state of Israel wasn't founded until a few years later, in 1948. It was even later than that, during the 1950s, that Israel sought reparations from Germany. The real clincher, though, is that those reparations were for the expenses Israel faced in providing a home for those Jews who'd been driven from Europe by the Nazi scourge, plus those who'd survived it but, not unnaturally, wanted to leave Europe for the new homeland. In other words, if finance had been the motive, it would have been in Israel's interests to pretend far more Jews survived the extermination campaign than was actually the case.

Leaving such details aside, how could anyone imagine it possible to maintain such a hoax?

A basic rule of logical reasoning is that, if all the evidence points in one direction, then that direction's probably the correct one. If all the people involved, from concentration-camp guards to concentration-camp inmates, say essentially the same thing, then we should need some persuading before we start to doubt them. If documentary evidence backs them up, our assumptions move toward cast-iron certainty. And if no one can give a plausible alternative answer to the question "Where *else* did six million Jews go?" . . .

One tactic of the Holocaust deniers has been to chip away at these individual strands of evidence separately. Is it not possible the Nazis at the Nuremberg Trials were confessing to crimes they hadn't committed in hopes of getting a lenient sentence? People who've lived for months or even years in the mind-destroying hell of a concentration camp might easily be confused in their recollections. The earlier histories of the Holocaust contain some errors that later historians have rectified—doesn't this mean we should doubt *everything* in those earlier histories?

All of these and many others like them are, taken individually, reasonable questions—at least on a superficial basis. On closer examination, however, most of the quibbles fall apart; for example, why would Nazis continue to say the Holocaust was real even after their death sentences had been handed down? More important, though, is that, even if one of the many lines of evidence pointing toward the reality of the Holocaust were proved completely false, all the rest would be unaffected. Yes, mainstream historians have had to make a few minor revisions to their earlier understanding; exactly zero of those revisions have come about because of the activities of the Holocaust deniers.

Let's look at one example of where the early Holocaust reporters seem to have got things wrong. During and immediately after World War II there were reports that the Nazis had manufactured soap from the corpses of their victims. Later evaluations suggest that, while a few Nazi psychopaths almost certainly did do this—Nazism was a political system in which psychopaths could thrive—there was never anything you might call *manufacture*. The error is one that the Holocaust deniers have pounced on. Of course, the error doesn't affect in any meaningful way the reality of the Holocaust.

A much later example of Holocaust-related error—although this time not historical error—concerned a 1992 poll that supposedly found a startling 22 percent of Americans who doubted the Holocaust had ever happened. Various theories were put forward as to how nearly one in five US citizens could possibly be so misguided. The pollsters took a more constructive approach. They looked again at the question that had elicited this odd result and realized it contained a double negative that was likely to confuse all concerned (pollsters included!). A 1994 follow-up indicated it was more like *two* percent who doubted the Holocaust. The episode was an example of rationalism working the way it should: An experiment (in this instance a poll) that produced an odd result was repeated, and the original results corrected.

Then there's the matter of the death toll. Some deniers claim the Holocaust is not so much a myth as an *exaggeration*: It wasn't six million Jews who died, just one million, or two million. That line of argument should be treated with the contempt it deserves. It's currently believed that the figure of six million is a reasonable estimate.

The leading Holocaust-denial organization, founded in 1978, is the Institute for Historical Review (IHR; not to be confused with the perfectly reputable Institute of Historical Research). Like so many "think tanks"—the Institute for Creation Research, the Discovery Institute, the Heartland Institute—the IHR has a name that gives the impression of academic sobriety while really just serving as a cover for a political agenda. Until 2002, the IHR published the *Journal of Historical Review;*

again, the title's deceptive, giving the impression that this was a properly peer-reviewed scholarly journal, while in fact there was no peer review. The IHR's origins were anti-Semitic, although in recent years it has attempted to disassociate itself from such views, or at least hide them under the guise of anti-Zionism.

Famously, in 1979, the IHR offered a $50,000 reward to anyone who could prove there had been gas chambers at Auschwitz used for the slaughter of human beings. Auschwitz survivor Mel Mermelstein gave eyewitness testimony that a court eventually decided was adequate proof, but the IHR simply ignored it. Mermelstein had to sue for the reward; the court told the IHR to pay the original $50,000 reward, plus an extra $40,000 for Mermelstein's "personal suffering."

Probably the best-known name associated with the IHR is that of the UK historian David Irving. Although he lacks academic training in history or even a degree (he twice reached university, first for physics and then for political economy, but both times ran out of money to continue), he made his name as a historian with his first book, *The Destruction of Dresden* (1963), about the carpet-bombing by the Allies of that historic German city. Up to 25,000 civilians died during what has more recently often been described as a war crime. At the time, the Nazis, for propaganda reasons, put the death toll at about 200,000, and the estimates Irving cited were more in line with this. Because his book was so successful, those grossly inflated estimates for a time became the accepted ones.

In 1993, Deborah Lipstadt published her book *Denying the Holocaust*,[1] and in it she accused Irving of, among other things, distort-

---

1. Still a standard work on the subject. The other relevant work of note is *Denying History* (2000), by Michael Shermer and Alex Grobman.

ing his evidence to make it fit a pro-Nazi ideology. In 1996–97 Irving indulged in a little flurry of libel suits against people critical of his work, and among these was a suit against Lipstadt and her UK publisher, Penguin Books. Because of the peculiarities of English libel law, the only defense Lipstadt and Penguin's lawyers could mount was a demonstration that, beyond reasonable doubt, her comments were factually correct. When the decision was handed down on April 11, 2000, the court declared that the defense had indeed done so on all substantive issues, the only two exceptions being trivia. Losing the case bankrupted Irving, who was ordered to pay most of the court costs, but, more than that, it made the UK public aware of his connection with far-right, neo-Nazi groups, and that the information in his books—hitherto usually shelved among orthodox histories—should be approached with caution.

Because his activities promoting Holocaust denial have been regarded as so inflammatory as likely to cause public unrest, Irving has been declared *persona non grata* in several countries, including Austria, Germany, Italy, and Canada.

Why do Holocaust deniers deny the best-documented event of the twentieth century? What drives them?

In some cases the answer is obvious: anti-Semitism, or even a misplaced reverence for the Nazis and their deeds. In others it seems it's the same motivation that can make people deny climate change or evolution: the instinctive belief that any self-evident fact is really just a concoction invented by authority as a means of controlling the public—in other words, a conspiracy. And in a few instances it appears the Holocaust deniers are in it just for the money: You can sell a lot of books and be paid handsomely for lectures to conspiracy theorists and anti-Semites!

AFROCENTRISM

In 1995, Mary Lefkowitz, a professor in the humanities at Wellesley College, spoke out against "Afrocentric" history, the growing inclination of African American historians to make false claims designed to glorify the role of black people. While equally detesting the habit that so many "mainstream" history books have of writing everyone except whites out of the picture, she couldn't stand by and allow these fresh falsehoods. As she said in her subsequent book, *Not Out of Africa* (1996):

> There is a current tendency . . . to regard history as a form of fiction that can and should be written differently by each nation or ethnic group. The assumption seems to be that somehow all versions will simultaneously be true, even if they conflict in particular details. According

Faking history in the cause of anti-Semitism is nothing new. Around 1900, there appeared in Russia a booklet called *The Protocols of the Elders of Zion*. It was supposedly the minutes of a meeting of senior rabbis as they plotted to take over the world through subversion of major national economies and the media. After a period of obscurity, it became popular among the Tsarist Russians, who blamed the Jews for their having lost the 1917 Revolution. The practice of equating communists with Jews and claiming a Jewish conspiracy of world domination to this line of argument, Afrocentric ancient history can be treated not as pseudohistory but as an alternative way of looking at the past. It can be considered as valid as the traditional version and perhaps even more valid because of its moral agenda.

Among the frequently repeated falsehoods that were being perpetrated in the name of Afrocentrism was that Aristotle stole his philosophy from books he found in the Library at Alexandria that had been written by black writers—tricky, because the library wasn't built until some decades after Aristotle's death!

Professor Lefkowitz was concerned about the promotion of fake history for ideological reasons. Just because much of the ideologically motivated fake history we come across in the US is born from white racism or pro-Christian prejudice doesn't mean everyone else should get a free pass to invent whatever history they want.

spread through Europe—where it guided in particular the Nazis—and even to the US, where such robust anti-Semites as Henry Ford spread the myth. In fact, not long after publication, the *Protocols* were shown to be a forgery, based partly on a French satire of Napoleon III and partly on some earlier anti-Semitic works of fiction. Even though it's perhaps the best-known forgery of the twentieth century, it's still taken seriously by a few obsessed anti-Semites. Few people swallow bullshit quite so readily as bigots.

REVISING CHRONOLOGY

There's a sense in which history can never be an exact science. Historians usually have to rely on what people wrote down at the time, and there are always plenty of reasons why contemporary writers might be putting a spin on things, or simply lying. Anyone will tell you that the Roman emperor Nero was a vile and sadistic mass murderer, for instance, but we "know" this based on the accounts of contemporary writers who all had good political reasons to hate his guts. We have no way of hopping into a time machine to go back and check the reality. Imagine you were a historian of the future and you were trying to work out what really happened in 2014 using transcripts from the cable news channels.

We also have to remember that it's only in relatively recent history that there have been good communications and a human lifespan as long as it has become; for example, when the earliest of the Christian gospels (Mark) was written, just a few decades after the events described, almost no potential eye-witnesses, even infants, would have still been alive. It's also only relatively recently that historians have thought it their duty to try to make their histories factually correct: For a long time it was thought quite respectable to fake history in order to glorify your current ruler, for example, or your culture.

What modern historians have to do is marshal all the evidence they can and see what it tells them as a whole. We know for sure that the Holocaust happened because all sorts of lines of independent evidence point toward that conclusion. But there are other areas in which our understanding is less assured. And, of course, it's still open to historians to interpret the evidence according to their own agenda.

But what if this were taken to extremes? What if historians of the past didn't just blur the details but actually invented whole swaths of what we now regard as reputable history? The twelfth-century British "historian" Geoffrey of Monmouth invented much of his *History of the Kings and Queens of England*, most famously King Arthur, Excalibur and the Knights of the Round Table. What if the French hero Charlemagne was similarly an invention?

This idea was put forward in the 1990s by the German writer Heribert Illig. Although Charlemagne has attracted legends in the same way that Arthur has, mainstream history has no doubt that he actually existed: He died in 814, having pulled together much of Western Europe, bringing it out of the barbarism it had largely endured since the fall of the Roman Empire. Illig and such disciples as Hans-Ulrich Niemitz, however, point to a number of apparent discrepancies in the orthodox histories of Europe and come to the conclusion that roughly three centuries—the years 614 to 911—were invented.

Illig supposes the Holy Roman Emperor Otto III and his mentor Gerbert of Aurillac, who in 999 (orthodox dating) became Pope Sylvester II, were the ones responsible. What if they were born not near the end of the tenth century but near the end of the seventh? Illig's idea is that between the two of them they decided it would be a great piece of PR if they were the ones on the two relevant thrones, secular and papal, when the millennium—the year 1000—came round. In order to engineer this, they rejigged the dating of the previous nine decades or so.

But wouldn't people *notice* if they went to bed in the late seventh century and woke up in the late tenth? We'd certainly notice if we were suddenly told it was the twenty-fourth century, not the twenty-first!

But, back then, there was no real reason for most people to register any disjunction. The BC/AD system of counting the years that we're accustomed to wasn't invented until the sixth century and didn't come into widespread use until about the time of the millennium. Even then, the general populace was more likely to reckon the passing of years (if at all) in terms of, for example, the reigns of current monarchs: "It happened during the sixth year of Pepin the Short . . ."

If we assume there was a plot—a conspiracy!—between Otto and Gerbert/Sylvester and that the dating was indeed reconfigured, we can imagine the consternation in the monasteries, which was where most of the chronicling of events was going on in Europe at the time. Suddenly chroniclers had three centuries of extra history in which, it seemed, *nothing had happened.* Those three centuries, of course, roughly coincide with what today we often call the Dark Ages, in part because we know relatively little about what went on.[1] To a monkish chronicler, the idea of three unaccounted-for centuries must have seemed anathema, yet at the same time who could doubt the decree of the emperor and pope? It would have seemed imperative to call upon divine inspiration to help *fill* those centuries with history—to reveal what had actually gone on, those events that somehow everyone had forgotten.

And thus the invention of Charlemagne.

If you restrict your study of the historical evidence to Western Europe, Illig's idea is very difficult to refute. It runs into major difficulties, however, when you try to correlate European chronologies with those from other cultures, like the Chinese and Arabic, whose histories show no corresponding disruption.

---

1. Historians generally now prefer to call it the Early Middle Ages.

Illig is not the only unorthodox scholar to have theorized that conventional historical chronologies are haywire. Another is the mathematician Anatoly T. Fomenko, who, with colleagues at the University of Moscow, from the 1980s onward produced papers and books contending that all of ancient history—the Egyptians, the Greeks, the Romans—actually happened in the Middle Ages, between about 1000 and 1500. The events of the New Testament came before those described in the Old Testament, which offers an easy explanation as to how the Old Testament prophecies about Christ were fulfilled!

A question arises: How do you jam thousands of years of documented history into a mere 500 years? The answer, according to Fomenko, is that there were far fewer historical events than we think there were. What we believe are cycles of historical events are really cases where several contemporary accounts of the same event have been later thought to apply to different ones. Historians, trying to fit all these supposedly separate events into their scheme of things, have assumed tracts of history that simply never existed. Those medieval monastic chroniclers played their part in forging history, as did the scholars of the Renaissance. Much of Russian history was more consciously faked in order to bolster the claims of the Romanov Dynasty to the imperial throne.

The theories of Fomenko and his colleagues are spelled out in a work translated into English as the multi-volume *History: Fiction or Science?* (2007–2008), totaling thousands of pages. These and other books by the Fomenko team promoting the "new chronology" are hugely popular and influential in Russia, although mainstream scholars both inside and outside the country dismiss them as rank pseudohistory.

Not all revisions of historical chronology belong so firmly on the fringes; some of them, after all, prove to be correct. The UK rock musician and Egyptologist David Rohl offers an example of what could be seen as a sort of halfway point between pseudohistory and the real stuff. During the 1990s, he proposed a redating of the reigns of the pharaohs of the 19th–25th Dynasties, a point of academic history that barely ruffled public awareness. Although his so-called New Chronology is disputed by most conventional Egyptologists, it's by no means impossible. More recently, however, he has claimed to have identified the location of the Garden of Eden.

Another person to have put forward a revised chronology for the ancient world was the Russian–American author Immanuel Velikovsky, who during the 1950s produced a series of bestselling books in which he rewrote much of physics and astronomy to, he believed, give credibility to events recorded in the Old Testament. In particular, he thought the planet Venus was born as a comet spat out by the giant planet Jupiter; on its way to the orbit it currently occupies, Venus swooped around the earth a few times, causing plagues and other nasty events that, according to Velikovsky, matched Old Testament and other ancient descriptions.

In order to get everything to fit in, Velikovsky had to redate events in Ancient Egypt and Ancient Israel, whose accepted chronologies, he came to believe, were out of sync with each other to the tune of several centuries. Like Fomenko later, he argued that one of the reasons for the supposed confusions in the orthodox chronology was that accounts from different cultures of a single individual could later be assumed to be of not one but several personages. Velikovsky spelled out his revised histories in *Ages in Chaos* (1952), his second 1950s blockbuster, and then in two much later volumes, *Peoples of the Sea* (1977) and *Ramses II and his Time* (1978).

The astronomer Carl Sagan once observed of Velikovsky's ideas that the astronomers thought the archaeology was pretty impressive but that the astronomy stank, while the archaeologists thought the astronomy looked plausible but the archaeology stank. It's always worth remembering that, no matter how distinguished someone's academic credentials are, when they're operating outside their own field of expertise they're no better off than the rest of us.

Velikovsky's academic training was as a psychiatrist.

FAKING US HISTORY

Revisionist history is by no means new to the US, but the past few years have seen a spate of attempts to rewrite not just recent events but those concerning the very birth of the nation. A particular bone of contention has been the First Amendment to the Constitution, which specifically forbids Congress to interfere in religious matters:

> Congress shall make no law respecting an establishment
> of religion, or prohibiting the free exercise thereof . . .

The Founders, whatever their own religious beliefs, quite clearly believed very strongly that the US should be a secular nation. One of those founders, Thomas Jefferson, made his views patent in his *Notes on the State of Virginia* (1782):

The legitimate powers of government extend only to such acts as are injurious to others. But it does me no harm for my neighbor to say there are twenty gods, or no god. It neither picks my pocket nor breaks my leg.

Such sentiments have not sat well with some among the dominant Christian community, who would like to see Christianity enshrined as the official state religion. When Jefferson ran for the US presidency in 1800, one of those who opposed him, a Reverend John M. Mason, declared that the quote above, which we might consider unexceptionable, indicated Jefferson was in favor of:

the morality of devils, which would break in an instant every link in the chain of human friendship, and transform the globe into one equal scene of desolation and horror, where fiend would prowl with fiend for plunder and blood.

Wow! And we thought Fred Phelps was bad.

Since turning the US into a Christian rather than a secular nation would be impossible without abolishing the First Amendment—a measure few sane politicians seem inclined to pursue—the alternative is to try to rewrite history in such a way as to claim that, whatever the *wording* of the First Amendment, the Founders *intended* this to be a Christian nation.

In the ringing statement of human rights that forms the second sentence of the Declaration of Independence, the Founders made plain their assumption that Judeo-Christian *morality* was a sort of universal standard:

We hold these truths to be self-evident, that all men are created equal, that they are endowed by their Creator with certain unalienable Rights, that among these are Life, Liberty and the pursuit of Happiness.

In 1776, in Colonial America, there were few who didn't believe there'd been a Creator of all things. Christianity was the majority religion among the colonists and their slaves, but many people, including several of the Founders and those around them, were Deists: they believed in God but rejected the rest of the paraphernalia of religion. The sentence quoted above was thus one that could be agreed by all concerned; it's certainly not one that could be used to justify a claim that Founders were trying to establish a Christian US.

Probably the most prominent writer at the moment trying to revise this history to make the Founders seem more Christian is the evangelical minister David Barton; like David Irving, although he's often referred to as a historian, he has no relevant professional qualifications. His background is primarily in religion, in Christian education and in politics.

Let's be clear on this matter of qualifications. If someone is doing research within the mainstream of historical studies, or if someone is merely popularizing history for general readers, the issue of professional qualifications is likely of secondary importance. Amateurs can do good historical research—in fact, where would the historical science of archaeology be without amateurs?—and, of course, there are plenty of popular history books and articles produced by people who're primarily writers and journalists, not historians. However, as in the sciences, if someone without qualifications and relevant experience is attempting to go against the conclusions of the professionals, the evidence they produce had better be pretty solid. It is not impossible that the amateur could be right and the professionals wrong, but only a fool would bet on it without exceptionally careful scrutiny.

In the scholarly world, the acid test of the worth of your work is, as we've seen (page 37), peer review. However, rather than submit his work for peer review, Barton formed the organization WallBuilders to publish and promote his writings and DVDs; there are also Wall-Builders Live radio broadcasts, likewise presenting his "historical" ideas while also attacking non-Christian elements of US society . . . such as environmentalism.

Huh?

Yes: Apparently environmentalism and efforts to resist climate change are anti-Christian. The logic seems to be that spending money to protect the environment harms the economy, which is contrary to the Bible's instructions to protect the poor. Presumably, the recommended way of protecting the poor is to let them die in mudslides or through drinking toxic water.

Barton's revisionist histories of the US and his works reinterpreting the motives of the Founders have been almost universally criticized by professional historians, including other Christian historians, on the grounds that the evidence he uses is often unreliable and his interpretations of it are often idiosyncratic. In 1995, after criticisms that he'd been inventing quotes or cherry picking them from dubious sources, he issued, through WallBuilders, a one-page statement called "Questionable Quotes": It comprised twelve quotations that Barton had attributed to the Founding Fathers and other historical figures in his lectures, videos, and books that he was now admitting were doubtful or false. Of course, the fact that for years he'd been putting these quotes out there means they've poisoned many people's understanding of their own history. After all, how often will someone watch a WallBuilders DVD and then go scour the internet in search of "Questionable Quotes"?

Many of the relevant quotes appeared in his book *The Myth of Separation* (1989), which sought to prove the Founders had never intended the separation of church and state. In the wake of his "Questionable Quotes" confession, that book was quietly revised for reissue as *Original Intent: The Courts, the Constitution and Religion* (1996). His book *The Jefferson Lies: Exposing the Myths You've Always Believed about Thomas Jefferson* (2012), which was for once released by a commercial publisher, became a *New York Times* bestseller before a readers' poll at the History News Network saw it receive the accolade of "least credible history book in print." At that point, his publisher very honorably withdrew the book, preferring the loss of revenue to the loss of integrity. In hindsight, the book's subtitle is deeply ironic.

Barton also has a decided political agenda. In 2010, for example, he advocated altering the Texas state social studies curriculum in public schools to remove Martin Luther King, Jr. from the textbooks. It is surely only because of this political agenda that he has been praised *as a historian* by figures like Glenn Beck, Newt Gingrich, Michele Bachmann, and Mike Huckabee, who famously described him as "maybe the greatest living historian on the spiritual nature of America's early days."

Eat your heart out, David Irving.

🚫

7. COPROLITE CLAIMS: FAKING ARCHAEOLOGY

Around 350 BCE, the Greek philosopher Plato wrote two treatises called *Timaeus* and *Critias*; they're usually called "dialogues" because he dressed up his philosophical essays as conversations between various stereotyped characters. In these two, he mentioned a great island civilization, Atlantis, that had been defeated by the Athenians. There's no reason to believe Plato meant Atlantis as anything more than a symbol—something he invented to boost Athenian pride and demonstrate the dangers of overconfidence—and for hundreds of years most people interpreted it that way. In the late nineteenth century, however, the US politician Ignatius Donnelly got it into his head that Plato was referring to a real place. Ever since the appearance of Donnelly's book *Atlantis: The Antediluvian World* in 1882, business has boomed for "unorthodox" archaeologists.

There is, of course, the possibility that Plato was basing his fiction on some genuine historical event. One idea that has supporters is that he incorporated legends of the collapse of the Minoan civilization, centered on the island of Crete, over a thousand years earlier. But what the amateur archaeologists are looking for is evidence and preferably relics of a major, technologically advanced civilization.

Donnelly himself thought Atlantis was the home of the Aryan master race (see page 44), who'd brought about the downfall of their civilization through a combination of promiscuity and warfare, yet were still our superiors. In the 1920s, Karl Georg Zschaetzsch agreed with him, but added some piquant details: Atlantis could be identified with the Garden of Eden, and everyone living there was vegetarian and teetotal (do you think this tells us anything about Zschaetzsch's own preferences?), but then a woman called Eve—non-Aryan, of course—introduced cider, the first time the Atlanteans had encountered booze. The downfall of their civilization was from that point inevitable but fun; what finally did it for them was when the earth was brushed by the tail of a comet. Just three Atlanteans/Aryans survived: the Teutonic god Wotan, his pregnant sister, and his daughter. Although the sister died in childbirth, the remaining Aryans enriched the human lineage by breeding with the shambling, non-Aryan primitives. Unfortunately, the Aryan strain was much diluted, which is why people today drink booze and eat meat.

Since Zschaetzsch's account mixed the Bible, the Aryans, and Teutonic myth, it's easy to see why the Nazis lapped it up!

But then there's the nineteenth-century amateur archaeologist Heinrich Schliemann. Despite general scholarly belief at the time that the Trojan war between the ancient Greeks and the city state of Troy was mere legend, Schliemann thought the events recounted in Homer's *Iliad* and Virgil's *Aeneid*, including that war, might have some historical basis. Ever since childhood he'd been obsessed with finding Troy, and in the 1870s he reckoned he'd found it in an archaeological site in northwestern Turkey. At the time his identification was accepted and, despite some dissenting voices, it still generally is.

We can see why amateur archaeologists tend to hold Schliemann up as a shining example. The trouble is, obviously, that just because *one* amateur archaeologist scored a major success doesn't mean it's a general pattern.

Among modern amateur archaeologists we have Graham Hancock. In his internationally bestselling book *Fingerprints of the Gods: A Quest for the Beginning and the End* (1995), Hancock proposed that at the end of the last glaciation, about 10,500 BCE, the continent of Atlantis sort of slid to the southern pole, where it now lies buried under the thick ice of Antarctica;[1] before the continent's demise, the Atlanteans passed on their science and technology to the Aztecs, Olmecs, Maya, and, on the other side of the Atlantic, the ancient Egyptians. Why didn't the Atlanteans, on realizing the end was nigh, simply emigrate? I don't know.

A different strain of spurious archaeology comes from the "researches" of Erich von Däniken and a slew of imitators who believe—or at the very least make lots of money claiming to believe—that thousands of years ago the earth was visited by travelers from the stars. These aliens interacted with our primitive ancestors and spurred the progress of early civilizations. A rhetorical trick used abundantly by von Däniken and many who've followed in his lucrative footprints is the making of statements like "There can be no other explanation for . . ."; lay readers have of course no way of knowing that professional archaeologists can offer copious explanations other than the one the author's giving.

Another rhetorical trick is to say on one page something like "Isn't it possible that the Egyptian pharaohs were mummified by alien 'gods' from a planet of the star Sirius?" and to follow this up a few pages later with: "As we've seen, the Egyptian pharaohs were mummified by alien 'gods' from a planet of the star Sirius." Unless you're paying careful attention to the text, it's easy to be fooled into thinking the author has built up a logical argument.

---

1. The way global warming's going, perhaps we'll soon rediscover it there.

Then there are bald statements that the average reader has no reason to suspect might just be plain false. A theme of von Däniken's is that our ancestors can't have been nearly as intelligent as orthodox archaeology tends to reveal them to have been. One aspect of this is his contention that the ancient Egyptians couldn't have erected the pyramids unaided: They must have had help from aliens zipping around on hovertrucks and using mighty energy beams to set the stones in place. Orthodox archaeologists have discovered enough ancient Egyptian science and technology to show the Egyptians were perfectly capable of doing the job, so von Däniken was forced to suggest they would have been hampered by their lack of wood and the technology to make rope. Again, archaeologists have discovered plenty of Egyptian rope and the Egyptians made widespread use of wood.

Von Däniken's speculations are by no means the wildest from the ancient-astronaut brigade. Another popular suggestion is that the alien visitors interbred with Neanderthals and the other pre-humans to produce *Homo sapiens*. But, bearing in mind that the aliens would have come from an evolutionary lineage completely different from ours, the chances of their being able to produce offspring with us would have been exactly zero. You have genetically far more in common with a jellyfish or a sphagnum moss than you could ever have with an extraterrestrial; how likely do you think it would be for you and a jellyfish or sphagnum moss to have children together?

In their book *Mystery of the Ancients* (1974), Craig and Eric Umland present the radical idea that the ancient Maya were explorers from a distant star. They initially made a base on the fifth planet—which lay between Mars and Jupiter—but, when this exploded, they settled on earth instead . . . although not before they had mined the metallic core of the moon. The proof of this latter contention is easy enough, the Umlands tell us: The moon doesn't have a metallic core any longer! There are two big flaws in this argument:

- It's the same as claiming we can tell the Maya ate all the cheese on the moon because there isn't any cheese there any longer.
- Actually, the moon *does* have a metallic core.

Seekers after evidence of Atlantis or ancient astronauts tend to keep a particular lookout for archaeological "anomalies"—artifacts that seem technologically far ahead of their time.

One such example is the Antikythera mechanism, a heavily corroded bronze device fished out of the Aegean Sea in 1900 and X-rayed in the 1970s. Although this is dated to the first century BCE, it's a navigational computer of a sophistication that wouldn't be matched again until the fourteenth century or later. Is it a relic of spacefaring aliens? Unlikely, because fourteenth-century technology wouldn't get you far if you were trying to mount an interstellar mission. Could it be based on Atlantean technology? If so, how come it was made centuries *after* the destruction of that supercivilization?

Or is the Antikythera mechanism simply evidence that the people of the ancient world were pretty smart? The astronomy on which it's based matches the level the Greek thinkers had achieved by about the first century BCE—a level far above any that'd be seen again in Europe until after the time of Copernicus. The ancient Greeks made all sorts of sophisticated machines; the big difference between the Antikythera mechanism and many of the others—which were essentially elaborate toys—is that the Antikythera mechanism had a definite practical use.

Another anomaly of interest appears to be the 65-million-year-old pyramid discovered in 2001 in Crimea by amateur archaeologist and dowser Vitali Goh.

Sixty-five million years old? That would date it back to about the time of the extinction of the dinosaurs, so if this were true there'd certainly have to be a major rewriting of the archaeology (and palaeontology) textbooks. Just before you get too excited, though, it's worth checking out the other achievements of Vitali Goh,[1] many of them based on his "method of geoholography and geohydrodiagnostics"— two of the "torsion technologies" that he has invented:

- The earth has a core that operates as a giant nuclear fusion reactor, creating all the elements, of the Periodic Table. (Even our neighboring giant nuclear fusion reactor, the sun, can't do that; for the heavier elements you need a supernova.)
- Mars is 70 percent diamonds, kimberlites, platinum, and gold, with oil and natural gas deposits far beneath the surface.
- The moon has a core of gold and platinum.
- And, oh yes, it's not just *one* ancient pyramid he's discovered in Crimea—it's 37 of them!

---

1. Or Vitaly A. Gokh, et cetera. There are various valid transliterations of his Cyrillic name.

THE PYRAMID INCH

Charles Piazzi Smyth, Scotland's Astronomer Royal for over twenty years in the latter part of the nineteenth century, was also interested in archaeology—in particular, in the Egyptian pyramids. He decided that 1/25 of the width of one of the Great Pyramid's casing stones must be a unit of measurement the pyramid builders used, and he called this the pyramid inch. Using this unit, he took all sorts of measurements in and around the Great Pyramid. He realized that, if you took the pyramid inch as a unit of *time*, too, the structure could be decoded as a sort of history book—and not just the history of the past, either: You could also read off predictions of the future!

What Smyth didn't realize was that the Great Pyramid's casing stones aren't all the same size, so . . .

You're there already, aren't you?

Smyth's investigations offer a classic example of confirmation bias (see page 77), a problem that plagues the field of unorthodox archaeology. When he was looking for measurements whose numerical value in pyramid inches would match significant historical dates, he found matches everywhere. With a different pyramid inch, none of those matches would have worked—but undoubtedly he'd have discovered lots of *other* matches to confirm his notion.

No wonder the bullshitters demand that orthodox science come clean about that 65-million-year-old pyramid—obviously there's a coverup going on.

The amateur collectors *par excellence* of such archaeological "anomalies" are two Krishna devotees, Michael A. Cremo and Richard L. Thompson. In their vast book *Forbidden Archaeology: The Hidden History of the Human Race* (1993)[1] they compile numerous examples of both artifacts and fossils being found in contexts that indicate wildly different dates from those the finds "should" have. Rather than causing sensations in the scientific community these "anomalies" have been — or so Cremo and Thompson believe—covered up by a sort of international scientific conspiracy not to rock the boat. Mainstream scientists, they reckon, are covering up that evolution doesn't work and that our deductions about ancient history are all wrong. Looking through the pair's books, we find a magnificent jumble, archaeological "anomalies" rubbing shoulders with tales of Bigfoot and the Abominable Snowman—tales that Cremo and Thompson accept with little question simply because, it seems, orthodox science rejects them.

Ask any archaeologist and they'll tell you there's plenty their profession doesn't know about the past, plenty of interesting mysteries still unsolved. The fake archaeologists would like you to believe they're offering solutions to these mysteries and many more, but in reality they're just muddying the water. Sometimes they're pretending there's a big hole in archaeological knowledge when in fact there isn't, like the "mystery" of the Egyptians and their rope. Other times there *is* genuinely a gap in archaeological knowledge; as always, just because we don't understand something doesn't mean we have to believe the first explanation that's offered us.

---

1. Even the condensed version they produced, *The Hidden History of the Human Race* (1994), is pretty formidable.

For example, sticking with the Egyptian pyramids, no one knows for sure *why* they were built. The unorthodox archaeologist might immediately fill this gap by telling you the Egyptians did it to satisfy some inscrutable whim of a race of now-vanished extraterrestrials. Yes, that is *an* explanation . . . but how likely is it to be the *right* one? Put it alongside one of the more rational speculations—a wealthy nation could afford to pay the laborers for these vast architectural projects, and it was in the nation's interests to do so because amply paid laborers spent their wages and so kept the national economy ticking over healthily—and it doesn't seem nearly so attractive, does it?

THE GREAT FLOOD

Legends about a great inundation in primordial times are found from all over the world, and this has often been taken to indicate that there actually *was* a worldwide flood. When looked at more closely, however, the flood legends from different parts of the world show different origins. The one we're familiar with from *Genesis* is a variant of the one found in an even older text, the *Epic of Gilgamesh*. Archbishop James Ussher, in constructing his chronology of Biblical events in the 1650s, set the date of the Flood as December 7, 2349 BCE, a Sunday.

When Ussher was doing his calculations, and for a couple of centuries afterward, it was generally assumed in Europe that the world was young. While it was obvious the earth had undergone very significant changes during its history, chronologies like Ussher's didn't allow the planet very *much* history—just a few thousand years. Thus many scientists reckoned the past must have been filled with catastrophic events that made major changes to the face of the earth very suddenly. This school of thought was called Catastrophism, and the Flood fit comfortably into its narrative.

There seemed to be good confirming evidence. Some rocks, called sedimentary rocks, showed layers, or strata, as if their material had settled out of water. Sometimes fossil fish and shells were found far away from the sea, even high in the hills; we now know movements of the earth's crust were responsible, but in the eighteenth century it seemed far more plausible those relics had been left there as the Flood's waters retreated. There were, too, what seemed to be old river valleys high in the mountains—in fact, valleys hewn out by glaciers that have since retreated.

During the nineteenth century, as it became obvious that the earth wasn't just a few thousand but at least many *millions* of years old, it became increasingly difficult to fit the Flood into the scheme of things. The bits of evidence that had seemed to favor a universal inundation were shown not just to have other explanations but to be from wildly differing dates. Those fossils, for example, are found in all sorts of different rock strata and so can't have been laid down at the same time—as we now know, they must have been laid down millions of years apart.

Also, people began to look more critically at the details of the *Genesis* account and realized that it couldn't be literally true. A boat the size of the Ark and built in the way described would soon fall apart on the open sea. The logistics of getting two of every kind of animal in the world aboard the vessel seemed inconceivable—and how would Noah have fetched the animals that lived in, say, Australia and South America? Why didn't the carnivorous animals eat the others? (A recent answer to this question has been that, before the Flood, all animals were herbivores. This doesn't help matters: How could the Ark hold all the

ARK-EOLOGISTS ON MOUNT ARARAT

- In 1876, an English historian, James Bryce, discovered a plank on Ararat and said it could only have come from the Ark.

- In 1892, a clergyman called Nouri told the world he'd not only found the Ark there but he'd been inside it and discovered it was exactly as described in *Genesis*. Sadly, there were no witnesses.

- An Armenian called Georgie Hagopian claimed in the 1970s that he and his uncle had discovered the Ark sometime before World War I. This account comes from *The Ark on Ararat* (1976), by Tim LaHaye and John Morris, a book that contains numerous other unsubstantiated claims of Ark discovery. (LaHaye would later be coauthor of the *Left Behind* series.) It seems incredible that neither the uncle nor any of his friends would have mentioned the Ark to the outside world and that, in the 1970s, Hagopian's recollection wouldn't have gone further than an overtly Christian publication.

- In 1952, French arkeologist Fernand Navar brought home a plank that was initially thought to be about 5,000 years old; later, radiocarbon dating showed it came from the middle of the seventh century. Various of Navarra's associates afterward declared he was a hoaxer, and had bought the plank elsewhere.

- In 2010, a group of Chinese and Turkish questers associated with the organization Noah's Ark Ministries International claimed that, in 2007 and 2008, they'd discovered seven big wooden sections in the ice high on the mountain. They went back in 2009 with a film crew and removed some wood which, they claimed, was radiocarbon dated to 4,800 years. One of the film crew assessed the situation: "[W]e think it is 99.9 percent that this is it." Noah's Ark Ministries International said the Turkish government was going to apply to have the site added to the UNESCO World Heritage list, but nothing seems to have come of that.

herb for the herbivores?) Think of the problem of clearing out all the animal poop. And so on.

All these considerations haven't stopped unorthodox archaeologists from mounting searches for the remains of the Ark—in much the same way as unorthodox zoologists mount searches for the Loch Ness Monster, but with, if anything, even less chance of success. And, just like their zoological counterparts, every now and then the ark-eologists declare success.

According to the *Genesis* account, the Ark came to rest on Ararat. This precision of location would seem to offer a big help in the hunt. Unfortunately, in biblical times the name "Ararat" referred not to what we now call Mount Ararat, but to more or less the whole of today's Armenia. The high, forbidding Caucasus mountains run right through the middle of Armenia; the thought that the Ark could be anywhere in that mountain chain is an intimidating one.

There's a tradition, though, that the *Genesis* account somehow *was* referring to Mount Ararat. This lies in Turkey, near the country's borders with Iran and Armenia, and is a formidable peak, the higher of its two summits reaching about 16,000 feet (about 5,000 meters) and being perpetually snow-covered. Not only would it be difficult to find the Ark in such terrain, just *being* there for any length of time is severely challenging. In more recent years a further difficulty has been that the mountain lies within a classified military zone.

YOUR PET DINO

There are dinosaurs all around you!

Well, not dinosaurs exactly, but their descendants: birds. Birds may not seem at a glance to look much like the lumbering monsters of the *Jurassic Park* movies, but if you get a chance to look at the skeleton of a crow or an eagle—or, really, just about any bird—you should soon spot the resemblance.

Leaving aside the birds, though, humans and dinosaurs have never coexisted. In fact, there's gap of over 60 million years between the extinction of the dinosaurs and the emergence of the first human beings.[1]

One of the difficulties faced by those unorthodox archaeologists who believe the earth is under 10,000 years old, and that life on earth was all

---

1. Crocodiles, however, were around at the time of the dinosaurs and looked in general much the same as they do now.

but extinguished by the Flood about 4,500 years ago, is trying to fit the dinosaurs into the scheme of things. Did they die out before the Flood? They can't have gone extinct *in* the Flood, because *Genesis* tells us Noah took two of every kind of living thing into the Ark. (It's difficult to know where he put the apatosaurs, but perhaps he simply took fertile eggs of the larger species.) Did the dinosaurs, then, die out *after* the Flood, for reasons unspecified? Whichever option we choose, the conclusion seems inevitable that at some stage humans and dinosaurs coexisted.

Most of the creationist archaeologists seem to opt for the dinosaurs having survived the Flood. Otherwise it would be difficult to explain those few instances of fossil dinosaur footprints—footprints laid down in clay that would have been washed away had the Flood's waters surged over them. So, if Archbishop Ussher's chronology is correct, dinosaurs were still extant as recently as about 2350 BCE.

This would mean they were still around at the time the ancient Egyptians were building the first pyramids—say, maybe *that's* how people were able to shift those huge stone blocks!—except that, of course, with so little post-Flood history to play with, you have to distort all our accepted chronologies of the ancient world in order to fit everything in. (The pyramid of Djoser, for example, is dated to about 2650 BCE, which is three centuries *before* Ussher's date for the Flood.)

It's the job of the creationist archaeologist, therefore, to look for signs of humans and dinosaurs interacting in some way. There are two possible approaches:

- Look for fossil evidence.
- Look for ancient cultural artifacts that depict dinosaurs.

In their book *The Genesis Flood* (1961), John C. Whitcomb Jr. and Henry Morris[1] claimed that fossilized human and dinosaur footprints could be found together in the bed of the Paluxy river, in Texas. The evidence could hardly have been clearer: Not only were there human and dinosaur trails, but in some places they overlapped in such a way that they must have been laid down at the same time. Even more excitingly, these weren't just any old human footprints: They were *giant* ones!

It seems Whitcomb and Morris based their claim on a 1939 article in the magazine *Natural History*, written by a certain Roland Bird. Bird's article was about the dinosaur footprints, which are fascinating in themselves. He added that tourists came from far and wide to see them and that the locals, recognizing the chance to make a quick buck, had manufactured the human prints.

The forgeries were pretty obvious, even to the eyes of creationist palaeontologists, although attempts were made to "explain" the discrepancies in terms of erosion. When that failed (how come the human footprints were "eroded" differently than the dino ones?), creationists combed the area looking for *other* fossilized human footprints. Sadly, this led them nowhere, and the third revised printing of *The Genesis Flood* quietly dropped the assertion. Other, more recent claims to have discovered human and dinosaur prints together have met a similar fate.

What about cultural artifacts, then?

If you go to a website like *Forbidden History* you'll find plenty of

---

1. Morris is regarded as one of the great pioneers of Creation Science, an attempt to make Creationism respectable—and hence suitable for teaching in school science classes. Eventually the courts decided the "Science" part of the name was a misnomer. Today, ID (see page 97) has taken over as the fake science that many Creationists seek to see taught in schools.

examples of ancient carvings and pictures that look a bit like they could be of dinosaurs.

As we've seen, one of the problems bedeviling unorthodox archaeologists is confirmation bias (see page 77). If you're looking at ancient carvings to see if any of them show dinosaurs, and you're convinced that some of them should, you'll eventually start seeing pictures of dinosaurs. Furthermore, if you put photographs of those carvings in a book or on a website where you're arguing that these are pictures of dinosaurs, *other people* will see them that way, too—they'll fall into the same confirmation-bias trap.

So it's very easy, if you go to a site like *Forbidden History*,[1] to see the "obvious" resemblances: you've been geared up to do so.

Then again, the skeletons of birds can look very much like those of dinosaurs. In very much the same way, a primitive carving of a bird could easily be mistaken for a depiction of a dino. Or the pictures could be of lizards: Those ancient carvings don't come with a scale attached, so what looks like a mighty *Tyrannosaurus rex* could actually be a lizard the length of the artist's finger.

And then there are outright forgeries. There's a place in Peru called Ica where thousands of stone carvings have been found that show not just humans interacting with prehistoric animals like dinosaurs but also all sorts of other "anomalous" items, like aerial maps. These were first brought to world attention by a physician called Javier Cabrera, who was given an Ica carving as a gift in 1961 and concluded the creature shown on it was a particular extinct species of fish. Fascinated, he told the locals he'd be interested to buy other examples of these ancient ar-

---

1. http://www.forbidden-history.com.

tifacts. Unsurprisingly, the locals started "discovering" lots of them for the rich doctor. Cabrera eventually put together a collection of about 10,000 carvings, some of which he believed to be as old as 13 million years—long before the appearance of *Homo sapiens*, according to conventional science. And it wasn't just dinosaurs the humans were interacting with. Elsewhere there were pictures of aliens . . .

It's easy to laugh at—and sympathize with—poor Cabrera. He was far from the first scholar to let his obsession blind him to the fact that he was being fooled by wily tricksters.

When you remove all the supposed dinosaur pictures that, like the Ica carvings, are known to be forgeries, plus all those that are more likely to be depictions of something else, like a bird or a lizard, there are still a few left over that definitely do have a sort of dinosaur look to them. How do we explain these?

The simple truth is that sometimes we just can't. Our ancestors came from cultures that were radically different from anything we know today, and some of the things they did are inexplicable to us. Without having a telepathic link to the brain of an artist who was working two thousand or five thousand or fifteen thousand years ago, we sometimes just don't know what a picture was supposed to represent. This doesn't mean we're declaring open season for interpreting ancient artworks.

Remember, extraordinary claims require extraordinary evidence. The idea that dinosaurs and humans coexisted is one of the more extraordinary of those "extraordinary claims"—it flies right in the teeth of many established, understood branches of science. It requires more to support it than just a few carvings that look kind of like dinosaurs but could be something else.

Here's a test for you. Imagine you're in a bookstore and you come across a fantasy novel with a picture of a unicorn on the cover.

Would you immediately assume that unicorns exist and the artist was painting from life? Of course not. You'd know the artist was perfectly aware this was a mythical creature.

Now imagine it's five thousand years in the future and you come across that same picture, which has miraculously survived. You no longer have the first idea of why the artist painted it.

Is the picture evidence that unicorns existed?

🚫

8. THE END OF THE WORLD WAS NIGH

In early 2014, media outlets like *World Net Daily* and Fox News—two organizations whose criterion of newsworthiness seems to be that it ain't news unless it's bullshit—were full of the latest end-of-the-world story. Relevant YouTube videos were going viral. If *World Net Daily* and Fox News were onto the story, could the History Channel be far behind? This time you felt that, unlike 2013, 2012, 2011, and all the other dead-certainty end-of-the-world dates, it was really going to be, well, *it*.

Or not, as the case might be.

Washington State Pastor Mark Biltz, author of the book *Blood Moons: Decoding the Imminent Heavenly Signs* (2013) and its accompanying DVD (both of which, by lucky happenstance, were for sale through the *World Net Daily* website), had been looking at the dates of upcoming total eclipses of the moon during 2014–15, and for some reason comparing these with the major Jewish holidays. Total lunar eclipses are sometimes called "blood moons" because (a) the moon's surface typically looks reddish-brown during them, and (b) the name helps sell sensationalist books to the gullible. What Pastor Biltz noticed was startling:

> . . . I was shocked to find that all four eclipses—over both years—fell on the biblical holidays of Passover and the Feast of Tabernacles. I just about jumped out of my skin.

Immediately I ran to my computer and pulled up NASA's website to look up other times when there have been four consecutive blood moons . . . NASA calls four total blood moons in a row a tetrad, and they list their occurrences. I noticed there weren't any in the 1600s, 1700s, or even the 1800s. The last time there was a tetrad was back in the 1900s, and to my amazement, they also fell on the feasts of Passover and Tabernacles.

Biltz was backed in his recognition that the four lunar eclipses heralded doom by no less an authority than Joseph Farah, founder of *World Net Daily*. Farah elucidated:

The wisdom of decoding these heavenly messages from our Creator in *Blood Moons* is overwhelmingly persuasive, and I believe this book will, for the first time, answer all the questions curious people of all walks of life will have about the imminent signs in the heavens. God is trying to get our attention. And I am convinced He has anointed Mark Biltz to help us understand the times in which we live and the urgent warnings God is trying to deliver to us all.

We should recognize a couple of things at the outset. First, lunar eclipses—which rely on the moon, sun, and earth being in a straight line, with the earth in the middle—can for obvious reasons occur only when the moon is full. Second, the Hebrew calendar is based on the cycles of the moon, and the Feast of Tabernacles (or Sukkot/Succot) and the start of

Passover are actually *defined* to fall on full moons. So the fact that a lunar eclipse should fall on a Jewish holiday is not in the slightest surprising.

We should also remember that lunar eclipses in general and total lunar eclipses in particular are not nearly so uncommon as their solar counterparts.[1] There are *at least* two lunar eclipses every year.

So, yes, it's moderately unusual that four lunar eclipses in a row will be total ones, but it's something less than boggling. It's by no means manifest that, in Biltz's words again:

> All these signs, coming together at one time, are poten-
> tially the culminating signals that God is closing this
> chapter of human history.

Biltz makes much of the fact that previous "tetrads" approximately match up with the establishment of modern Israel (1948) and the annexation of East Jerusalem by Israel during 1967's Six-Day War. But this kind of matching up is easy—far too easy. Wherever in history you find a quartet of total lunar eclipses, you're sure to be able to spot some major historical event, somewhere in the world, that occurred at roughly the same time—especially since the four eclipses concerned must necessarily be spread out over eighteen months or so.

Finally there's the odd notion that God is trying to communicate with us by setting up the four eclipses. Any competent astronomer could have sat down a century or more ago and, using tables of lunar eclipses

---

1. A lunar eclipse happens when the moon goes into the earth's shadow. A solar eclipse happens when (a part of) the earth goes into the moon's shadow. The earth, being a far bigger object than the moon, casts a far bigger shadow. The bigger the shadow, the more likely something is to pass through it.

then available, predicted precisely the dates on which these four "blood moons" would fall. No special intervention by God has been required: They were going to happen anyway. That's the wonder of physics!

Besides, why would God be in the business of "trying" to deliver "urgent warnings" (Farah's words) to us? Surely, if an omnipotent God wanted to get a message through to us, He'd be uniquely placed to make sure there was no error in transmission. Why should He be fooling around with lunar eclipses when there are about a gazillion vacant cable TV channels open to Him?

The clincher for *World Net Daily* came on February 16, a few days after their first report, when someone noticed the NASA eclipses site had been taken down for maintenance. Despite the fact that NASA had posted a link so that people could in the interim go to the US Naval Observatory website to find the identical information, *World Net Daily* knew *exactly* what was going on.

A government coverup!

APPROACHING THE MILLENNIUM

The idea that the end of the world is imminent is almost as old as the Christian tradition. All three of the gospels according to Matthew, Mark, and Luke record Christ saying that some of those listening to him "would not taste death" (i.e., would still be alive) by the time his Second Coming came around. It seems his followers took him literally at the time; it was only after a few decades that efforts started to reinterpret the remark as a metaphorical one; an alternative explanation has been that what Christ *really meant* was that some of the disciples would witness his resurrection.

Other religions have had similar ideas about the end of the world. In the Jewish apocalyptic tradition, for example, it's believed the era in which we live, dominated as it is by evil, will one day be supplanted by a second period of history, which will be under the beneficent rule of YHWH, the transition being marked by the intervention of a messiah.

The eleventh-century French monk Rodulfus (or Raoul, or Ralph) Glaber wrote a history in which he recorded that, as the year 1000 approached, there had been widespread fear that the ending of the millennium would be marked by the Second Coming. This seems to have been a myth, or almost entirely so. Aside from anything else, at the time almost nobody outside the monasteries (and even within them) followed the AD system of numbering years. The vast majority of people didn't have a clue that the first millennium was about to end, and probably would have been unimpressed even if they *had* known.

Nineteenth-century historians took Glaber's account of millennium panic seriously, and through much of the twentieth century, history textbooks treated it as a fact. It wasn't really until the approach of the year 2000 that the misconception was scrubbed from popular imaginings . . . just in time for various fringe sects to start panicking about the end of the *second* millennium. However, the year 2000 arrived without mishap, and so did the year 2001 (the millennium really began with January 1, 2001). Of greater concern was the so-called Year 2K Bug; in the early days of computing, programmers had shortsightedly utilized date-counters that ran only up to 1999, and some people worried that a sort of grand cybernetic breakdown at the instant 1999 gave way to 2000 would lead to the collapse of modern technological civilization. But Y2K proved to be another damp squib.

After all the many failed predictions, it seems it's reasonable to ask the question: "When did the world end?"

It can sometimes be hard to tell. The Anglo-Israelite sect predicted, on the basis of measurements made in the Great Pyramid, that the world would end in 1936; in 1940 the date was amended to 1953; in 1953 it was announced that the world *had* ended, but that no one except believers had noticed it. It will be, they claimed, a while before the effects become manifest. This notion—that doomsday came and went without anyone except the faithful realizing it—has not been unique to the Anglo-Israelites: Hiram Edson made it a tenet of the Seventh Day Adventist movement that the world had ended in 1844, as predicted by his mentor William Miller.

Others faced with the dilemma of a predicted Armageddon having been a little on the quiet side have adopted a different approach: They have reinterpreted—or, as some might put it, changed—the original apocalyptic prediction. Wilbur Glenn Voliva—a major US cult leader of the early twentieth century who preached that the earth was flat—told his followers the world would end in 1923, 1927, 1930, and then 1935; he was doubtless much disillusioned by the time he died in 1942.

While many world's-end predictions have had religious motivations—even if the religion involved is nothing the established faiths would recognize—until relatively recently the assumption that the end of the world was imminent could be *scientifically* respectable. After all, if the earth had existed for only a few thousand years and was already past its prime, surely it couldn't go on much longer. Often enough, the perceived "change and decay" was sufficiently obvious for people to expect the Second Coming must be soon. They may have been reassured by Sir Isaac Newton's calculation, based on the Bible, that the end couldn't come until at least 2060.

Long after such quasi-science had been abandoned by rationalists, it persisted in the minds of the credulous. To pick just a single example, in a 1977 document issued by the fundamentalist Worldwide Church of God we find that:

> . . . God has allotted mankind 6,000 years in which to *learn* that the ways of man bring nothing but SUFFER-ING and DEATH! . . . human life may have begun on this earth 4,004 B.C. (Other evidence indicates it may have been a little earlier.) . . . How awe-inspiring and significant that in OUR PRESENT AGE—in the very time that the world is threatened with the extinction of all life—6,000 years have *almost elapsed*.

CAMPING OUT

Today, belief in the imminence of the Secret Rapture, precursor of the Second Coming, is widespread in the US. Far from being, as many think, a biblical prophecy, the notion of the Rapture was invented as recently as 1832 by John Nelson Darby, a pioneer of the Plymouth Brethren sect, and spread by the Irish evangelist William Kelly. Darby imagined Christ making a preliminary foray to the earth to gather up the souls of the faithful, living or dead, and take them to Heaven for safekeeping through all the vicissitudes of Armageddon; thereafter, those souls would return here alongside Christ for the Second Coming. The popularity of the Rapture has been vastly increased by the *Left Behind* book series written by Tim LaHaye and Jerry B. Jenkins.

Harold Camping, president of the evangelical media company Family Radio, had a habit of predicting the end of the world as we know it. In his book *1994?* (1992) he predicted the Last Judgment would arrive in September 1994—although, to be fair, he did say this was only a strong likelihood, not a certainty.

September 1994 came and went without undue alarm. Soon Camping was making his predictions again, this time setting them a safer distance into the future. The chosen year, according to Camping's further analysis of biblical passages, was now 2011, with the Rapture occurring on May 21 and the final fireworks on October 21.

In the early months of 2011, Camping's prediction was fodder for comedians and cartoonists—not to mention the general public—all over the world. Unfortunately, though, there were plenty of people who believed him. Reports came in from all over of people selling up their property to give money to Christian organizations, notably to Family Radio's campaign to spread word of the imminent Rapture. Families fell apart when, for example, young people discovered their parents had just cashed out the college fund. There were a number of suicides, presumably of people who just couldn't wait for May 21 to roll around.

Alas, May 22 rolled around, too.

On May 23 Camping told the world he'd gotten it wrong. There *had* been a version of the Rapture on May 21, but it had been a spiritual rather than a physical one, so people had tended not to notice it. Both Rapture and Final Trump,[1] he now clarified, would arrive in rapid succession on October 21. In the meantime, Family Radio would hang on to all the donations it had received.

---

1. No relation to Donald.

Confounding expectations, October 22 arrived.

This time Camping washed his hands of further end-times predictions, and a couple of years later he died. However, just before we dismiss him as a lone crackpot it's worth noting that his company, Family Radio, according to figures submitted to the IRS for the year 2009, pulled in $18,358,350 in contributions for that year alone and was valued at $72 million. Predicting the end of the world can be big business.

2012 AND ALL THAT

Another set of end-of-the-world predictions to make international headlines concerned the Mayan calendar, whose most recent cycle concluded on December 22, 2012. What the Maya predicted for the end of time makes the contents of *Revelation* pale by comparison, so one can understand the nervousness. It tended to go ignored that 2012 would mark only, as stated, the end of one of the calendar's cycles; the calendar's predicted end of the world isn't until the 50th century.

Even so, the excitement built among the doomsayers, with other predictors zeroing in on 2012—the period December 21–23 being the most popular. In his *Fingerprints of the Gods* Graham Hancock, following in the footsteps of Charles Piazzi Smyth (see page 250), demonstrated how Pyramid measurements pointed to December 23 as the world's last day. Or perhaps his pyramidological prophecy really coincided with the Mayan one? After all, December 22 and December 23 can be the same day for people on the two different sides of the International Date Line.

An end of the world on December 22 or 23 was all very well, but the calculating savants were assuming we'd survived December 21!

This was the end-day predicted by the "psychonaut" Terence Kemp McKenna—originator of the Stoned Ape Theory of human evolution, whereby our ancestors became distinct from the other primates through the ready availability in their region of psychedelic mushrooms.[1] His cosmological Novelty Theory envisaged time having a wave structure, bringing moments of enhanced extropy (the opposite of entropy) to the universe. Plotting the necessary graphs, he concluded that his math matched that of the Maya—to the nearest day or so, anyway.

Less date-specific predictions of doom for 2012 abounded, among them that of Michael Drosnin, author of the bestseller *The Bible Code* (1997), in which he claimed to have been able to decipher all sorts of coded messages hidden in the Bible that no one else had noticed before. He discovered a clear indication in the holy text that the earth was going to be hit by a comet in 2012.

Meanwhile, in *Serpent of Light: Beyond 2012* (2008), the "spiritual teacher" Drunvalo Melchizedek (formerly known as Bernard Perona) told how our planet's Kundalini—or Serpent of Light—shifts its position every 13,000 years, and the next shift was due in 2012.

For all of these reasons, January 1, 2013, came as quite a surprise to many.

Of course, the survival of the world past 2012 doesn't mean the predictions will stop. As we've seen, the game is now on for 2014/2015. And, after the "blood moons" have failed to deliver, there'll undoubtedly be something else.

---

1. Psilocybin mushrooms, often called magic mushrooms, have been valued since ancient times because they contain hallucinogenic drugs.

BANG OR WHIMPER?

The *real* end of the world will come in several billion years' time, when the planet's orbit will have sufficiently decayed for it to plunge into a by then mightily bloated sun. One way or another, the human species will long have disappeared by that time. The end of the world as we know it—in other words, the collapse of our current civilization—is a far more immediate concern.

Uncurbed climate change could well bring it about within decades; or a meteor impact of the size of the one that did for the dinosaurs could happen next week. About the latter threat we can obviously do nothing (although people are working on it). About the former, we can, each and every one of us, do at least *something*.

A good start is to counter the bullshit that's being cynically spread throughout our culture by the professional climate change denialists. They may take offense (or pretend to) if you denounce their bullshit robustly—they may even complain about your use of the word "bullshit"—but don't worry. Simply by delaying action on climate change, they're demonstrating that they don't care if you live or die.

Alongside that stark fact, who cares about their hurt feelings?

Welcome to the War on Bullshit.

🚫

BIBLIOGRAPHY

Agin, Dan. *Junk Science: An Overdue Indictment of Government, Industry, and Faith Groups that Twist Science for Their Own Gain*. New York: Thomas Dunne Books, 2006

Ariely, Dan. *Predictably Irrational: The Hidden Forces that Shape Our Decisions*. New York: Harper, 2008

Angell, Marcia. *Science on Trial: The Clash of Medical Evidence and the Law in the Breast Implant Case*. New York: Norton, 1996

Ayala, Francisco J. *Darwin's Gift to Science and Religion*. Washington DC: Joseph Henry Press, 2007

Bartholomew, Robert E., and Radford, Benjamin. *Hoaxes, Myths, and Manias: Why We Need Critical Thinking*. Amherst: Prometheus, 2003

Bartholomew, Robert E., and Radford, Benjamin. *The Martians Have Landed!: A History of Media-Driven Panics and Hoaxes*. Jefferson, McFarland, 2012

Black, Edwin. *War Against the Weak: Eugenics and America's Campaign to Create a Master Race*. New York: Four Walls Eight Windows, 2003

Brookes, Martin. *Extreme Measures: The Dark Visions and Bright Ideas of Francis Galton*. London: Bloomsbury, 2004

Carroll, Sean B. *The Making of the Fittest: DNA and the Ultimate Forensic Record of Evolution*. New York: Norton, 2006

Collins, Loren. *Bullspotting: Finding Facts in the Age of Misinformation*. Amherst: Prometheus, 2012

Coontz, Stephanie. *The Way We Never Were: American Families and the Nostalgia Trap*. New York: Basic Books, 1992

Coyne, Jerry A. *Why Evolution is True*. New York: Viking, 2009

Davies, Nick. *Flat Earth News: An Award-Winning Reporter Exposes Falsehood, Distortion and Propaganda in the Global Media*. London: Chatto & Windus, 2008

Dawkins, Richard. *The Blind Watchmaker: Why the Evidence of Evolution Reveals a Universe Without Design*. New York: Norton, 1986

Dawkins, Richard. *The Greatest Show on Earth: The Evidence for Evolution*. New York: Free Press, 2009

de Camp, L. Sprague. *The Ragged Edge of Science*. Philadelphia: Owlswick, 1980

Desmond, Adrian, and Moore, James. *Darwin's Sacred Cause: How a Hatred of Slavery Shaped Darwin's Views on Human Evolution*. Boston: Houghton Mifflin Harcourt, 2009

Ekman, Paul. *Telling Lies: Clues to Deceit in the Marketplace, Politics, and Marriage*, revised edition. New York: Norton, 2009.

Evans, Christopher. *Cults of Unreason*. London: Harrap, 1973

Feder, Kenneth L. *Frauds, Myths, and Mysteries: Science and Pseudoscience in Archaeology*, third edition. Mountain View CA, Mayfield, 1999

Feldman, Robert. *The Liar in Your Life: The Way to Truthful Relationships*. New York: Twelve, 2009

Flank, Lenny. *Deception by Design: The Intelligent Design Movement in America*. St. Petersburg, Red and Black, 2007

Frazier, Kendrick. *Science Under Siege: Defending Science, Exposing Pseudoscience*. Amherst: Prometheus, 2009

Gardner, Martin. *Fads and Fallacies in the Name of Science*. New York: Dover, 1957

Gardner, Martin. *The New Age: Notes of a Fringe Watcher*. Buffalo: Prometheus, 1988

Gardner, Martin. *Science: Good, Bad and Bogus*. Amherst: Prometheus, 1989

Gardner, Martin. *Did Adam and Eve Have Navels? Debunking Pseudoscience*. New York: Norton, 2000

Gelbspan, Ross. *Boiling Point: How Politicians, Big Oil and Coal, Journalists, and Activists Have Fueled the Climate Crisis—and What We Can Do to Avert Disaster*. New York: Basic Books, 2004

Goldacre, Ben. *Bad Science*, revised edition. London: Fourth Estate, 2009

Goldsmith, Donald (editor). *Scientists Confront Velikovsky*. New York: Norton, 1977

Gore, Al. *The Assault on Reason*. New York: Penguin, 2007

Grant, John. *Discarded Science: Ideas that Seemed Good at the Time*. London: AAPPL, 2006

Grant, John. *Corrupted Science: Fraud, Ideology and Politics in Science*. London: AAPPL, 2007

Grant, John. *Bogus Science: Some People Really Believe These Things*. Wisley: AAPPL, 2009

Grant, John. *Denying Science: Conspiracy Theories, Media Distortions, and the War Against Reality*. Amherst: Prometheus, 2011

Gratzer, Walter. *The Undergrowth of Science: Delusion, Self-Deception and Human Frailty*. Oxford: OUP, 2000

Harrison, Guy P. *50 Popular Beliefs that People Think Are True*. Amherst: Prometheus, 2012

Heard, Alex. *Apocalypse Pretty Soon: Travels in End-Time America*. New York: Norton, 1999

Hoggan, James, with Littlemore, Richard. *Climate Cover-Up: The Crusade to Deny Global Warming*. Vancouver: Greystone, 2009

Huber, Peter W. *Galileo's Revenge: Junk Science in the Courtroom*. New York: Basic Books, 1993

Hughes, Richard T. *Myths America Lives By*. Urbana and Chicago: Illinois University Press, 2003

Jacoby, Susan. *The Age of American Unreason*. New York: Pantheon, 2008

Jennings, Ken. *Because I Said So: The Truth Behind the Myths, Tales, and Warnings Every Generation Passes Down to Its Kids*. New York: Scribner, 2012

Kaminer, Wendy. *Sleeping with Extra-Terrestrials: The Rise of Irrationalism and Perils of Piety*. New York: Pantheon, 1999

Kaplan, Michael, and Kaplan, Ellen. *Bozo Sapiens: Why to Err is Human*. New York: Bloomsbury, 2009

Kasten, G. Randy. *Just Trust Me: Finding the Truth in a World of Spin*. Wheaton: Quest, 2011

Kitcher, Philip. *Abusing Science: The Case Against Creationism*. Cambridge: MIT Press, 1982

Krauss, Lawrence. *A Universe from Nothing: Why There is Something Rather than Nothing*. New York: Free Press, 2012

Kusche, Larry. *The Bermuda Triangle Mystery—Solved*, revised edition. Buffalo: Prometheus, 1986

Lefkowitz, Mary. *Not Out of Africa: How Afrocentrism Became an Excuse to Teach Myth as History*. New York: New Republic/Basic, 1996

Lipstadt, Deborah E. *Denying the Holocaust: The Growing Assault on Truth and Memory*. New York: Free Press, 1993

Livingston, James D. *Driving Force: The Natural Magic of Magnets*. Cambridge: Harvard University Press, 1996

Loewen, James W. *Lies My Teacher Told Me: Everything Your American History Textbook Got Wrong*. New York: New Press, 1995

Mitroff, Ian I., and Bennis, Warren. *The Unreality Industry: The Deliberate Manufacturing of Falsehood and What It Is Doing to Our Lives*. New York: OUP, 1989

Monbiot, George. *Heat: How to Stop the Planet Burning*. Cambridge: South End Press, 2007

Mooney, Chris. *The Republican War on Science*. New York: Basic Books, 2005

Mooney, Chris, and Kirshenbaum, Sheril. *Unscientific America: How Scientific Illiteracy Threatens Our Future*. New York: Basic Books, 2009

Moreno, Jonathan D. *The Body Politic: The Battle Over Science in America*. New York: Bellevue Literary Press, 2011

Nattrass, Nicoli. *Mortal Combat: AIDS Denialism and the Struggle for Antiretrovirals in South Africa*. Scottsville: University of KwaZulu–Natal Press, 2007

Niewyk, Donald, and Nicosia, Francis. *The Columbia Guide to the Holocaust*. New York: Columbia University Press, 2000

Offit, Paul A. *Autism's False Prophets: Bad Science, Risky Medicine, and the Search for a Cure*. New York: Columbia University Press, 2008

Offit, Paul A. *Deadly Choices: How the Anti-Vaccine Movement Threatens Us All*. New York: Basic Books, 2011

Offit, Paul A. *Do You Believe in Magic?: The Sense and Nonsense of Alternative Medicine*. New York: HarperCollins, 2013. (UK edition retitled *Killing Us Softly: The Sense and Nonsense of Alternative Medicine*)

Oreskes, Naomi, and Conway, Erik M. *Merchants of Doubt: How a Handful of Scientists Obscured the Truth on Issues from Tobacco Smoke to Global Warming*. New York: Bloomsbury, 2010

Park, Robert L. *Voodoo Science: The Road from Foolishness to Fraud*. Oxford: OUP, 2000

Park, Robert L. *Superstition: Belief in the Age of Science*. Princeton: Princeton University Press, 2008

Peters, Shawn Francis. *When Prayer Fails: Faith Healing, Children, and the Law*. Oxford: OUP, 2008

Press, Bill. *Spin This! All the Ways We Don't Tell the Truth*. New York: Pocket, 2001

Prothero, Donald R. *Reality Check: How Science Deniers Threaten Our Future*. Bloomington & Indianapolis: Indiana University Press, 2013

Randi, James. *Flim-Flam!: The Truth about Unicorns, Parapsychology, and Other Delusions*. New York: Lippincott & Crowell, 1980

Randi, James. *The Mask of Nostradamus: A Biography of the World's Most Famous Prophet*. New York: Scribner, 1990

Rees, Martin. *Just Six Numbers: The Deep Forces that Shape the Universe*. London: Weidenfeld & Nicolson, 1999

Sagan, Carl. *The Demon-Haunted World: Science as a Candle in the Dark*. New York: Random House, 1995

Schick, Theodore, and Vaughn, Lewis. *How to Think About Weird Things: Critical Thinking for a New Age*, seventh edition. New York: McGraw-Hill, 2013

Schwarcz, Joe. *Science, Sense and Nonsense: 61 Nourishing, Healthy, Bunk-Free Commentaries on the Chemistry that Affects Us All*. Toronto: Doubleday Canada, 2009

Shanks, Niall. *God, the Devil, and Darwin: A Critique of Intelligent Design Theory*. Oxford: OUP, 2006

Shermer, Michael. *Why People Believe Weird Things: Pseudo-Science, Superstition, and Bogus Notions of Our Time.* New York: Freeman, 1997

Shermer, Michael. *The Borderlands of Science: Where Science Meets Nonsense.* New York: OUP, 2001

Shermer, Michael, and Grobman, Alex. *Denying History: Who Says the Holocaust Never Happened and Why Do They Say It?* Berkeley: University of California Press, 2000

Shubin, Neil. *Your Inner Fish: A Journey into the 3.5-Billion-Year History of the Human Body.* New York: Pantheon, 2008

Singh, Simon, and Ernst, Edzard. *Trick or Treatment: Alternative Medicine on Trial.* London: Bantam, 2008

Snowden, Frank M. Jr. *Before Color Prejudice.* Cambridge: Harvard University Press, 1983

Specter, Michael. *Denialism: How Irrational Thinking Hinders Scientific Progress, Harms the Planet, and Threatens Our Lives.* New York: Penguin, 2009

Taibbi, Matt. *The Great Derangement: A Terrifying True Story of War, Politics, and Religion at the Twilight of the American Empire.* New York: Spiegel & Grau, 2008

Thompson, Damian. *Counterknowledge: How We Surrendered to Conspiracy Theories, Quack Medicine, Bogus Science, and Fake History.* New York: Norton, 2008

Toumey, Christopher P. *God's Own Scientists.* New Brunswick: Rutgers University Press, 1994

Wanjek, Christopher. *Bad Medicine: Misconceptions and Misuses Revealed, from Distance Healing to Vitamin O.* Hoboken: Wiley, 2003

Wheen, Francis. *How Mumbo-Jumbo Conquered the World: A Short History of Modern Delusions.* London: Fourth Estate, 2004

Wicker, Christine. *Not in Kansas Anymore: A Curious Tale of how Magic is Transforming America.* San Francisco: HarperSanFrancisco, 2005

INDEX

Mystery of the Ancients (Umland), 247–248
Myth of Separation, The (Barton), 243

Nader, Ralph, 140
Napoleon III, 233
NASA, 62, 222–223, 263, 265
National Center for Complementary and Alternative Medicine (NCCAM), 143
National Climatic Data Center, 206, 208
National Institutes of Health, 143
National Resources Defense Council (NRDC), 210
National Science Board, 23
Native Americans, 81
Nativity, 24
Natural History, 258
natural phenomena, 117–118
natural selection, 49–50, 90–91, 98
Natural Theology, or Evidence of the Existence and Attributes of the Deity Collected from the Appearances of Nature (Paley), 97–98
naturalists, 98
Nature, 134
nature, laws of, 22
Navar, Fernand, 254
Nazi Germany, 44–46, 81, 107, 109
Nazis, 226–233
NBC, 195
Neanderthals, 107, 247
needles, 34-35, 150-152
Neomax magnets, 158–159
neo-Nazi groups, 231
Nero, 234
neurosurgeons, 28
neurotoxicants, 176, 180
New York Times, 243
Newcomb, Simon, 125
Newsweek, 205
Newton, Sir Isaac, 57–58, 69, 71, 221, 223, 267
Niemitz, Hans-Ulrich, 235
Nigeria, 179
Noah, 24, 104

Noah's Ark, 87, 104, 253, 254–255, 257
Noah's Ark Ministries International, 255
Nostradamus, 115, 133
Not Out of Africa (Lefkowitz), 232–233
Nouri, 254
Novelty Theory, 271
"Nun's Priest's Tale, The" (Chaucer), 114
Nuremberg Trials, 227
nutritionists, 37
Nye, Bill, 87, 92

Obama, Barack, 25–27, 81, 220
Obamacare, 118
"Objections to Astrology," 129
objectivity, 77, 84
obscure information, 56
oceans, 188–189, 201
oil, 22, 193-194, 219
oil companies, 22
Old Testament, 57–58, 237-238
old-earth Creationists (OECs), 111
O'Reilly, Bill, 63–64
organization, 93–94
Origin of Species (Darwin), 49–50, 53–54
Original Intent: The Courts, the Constitution and Religion (Barton), 243
Otto III, 235–236
outer space, 96–102
oxygen, 198, 207-209
ozone layer, 107, 188-189, 200, 211

Pakistan, 179
Paley, William, 97–98
Palin, Sarah, 215–216
paradigm shift, 71
parapsychology, 127-128, 130-131
Parapsychology Laboratory (Duke University), 127
Passover, 262, 263–264
Pasteur, Louis, 156
patterns, 79–80
Pauling, Linus, 155
Paulos, John Allen, 115

peer reviews, 72
Penguin Books, 231
Pentagon, 219
Peoples of the Sea (Velikovsky), 239
peppered moths, 91
permafrost, 201-202
Perona, Bernard, 271
Peterson, Thomas, 206
Pharyngula, 123
Phelps, Fred, 240
Phillips, Peter, 130–131
physics, 63, 149, 238
Pink Panther, 34
Pithovirus sibericum, 202
placebo effect, 144–145, 147, 151–152
plagiarism, 73
plate tectonics, 71
Plato, 244
pneumonia, 32–33
polar vortex, 183–190
polio, 34, 177, 179
political ideologies, 21, 22–23
politics, 53–54, 66, 211
polls. See surveys
polyethylene glycol, 174
Pope Paul VI, 115
Pope Sylvester II, 235–236
Popper, Karl, 68
population sizes, 108, 193
populations, 109
Post, 205
power, abuse of, 29–30
Power, Tyrone, 154
prayer, 32, 34, 114, 119–123
preconceived ideas, 76
predictions, 69, 111, 115-116, 266–271
pregnancy, 36
prerecognition, 127
primates, 95–96
Principles of Biology (Spencer), 110
prison, 39–42
Proctor, Bob, 112
projection, 64
promiscuity, 35
proof by intimidation, 56–58
Protocols of hte Elders of Zion, The, 232
psychiatry, 155
psychic detectives, 117–118
psychic phenomena, 125
"psychic research," 127